W9-BGY-828

GARDENS FOR OUTDOOR LIVING

COMPLETE GARDENER'S LIBRARY™

GARDENS FOR OUTDOOR LIVING

A. Cort Sinnes

National Home Gardening Club
Minnetonka, Minnesota

GARDENS FOR OUTDOOR LIVING

Copyright © 2001 National Home Gardening Club

All rights reserved. No part of this publication may be reproduced, stored in an electronic retrieval system or transmitted in any form or by any means (electronic, mechanical, photocopying, recording or otherwise) without the prior written permission of the copyright owner.

Mike Vail
Vice President, Product & Business Development

Tom Carpenter
Director of Book Development

Dan Kennedy
Book Production Manager

Michele Teigen
Senior Book Development Coordinator

Gina Germ
Photo Editor

Circus Design
Book Production & Design

1 2 3 4 5 / 05 04 03 02 01
ISBN 1-58159-081-4

National Home Gardening Club
12301 Whitewater Drive
Minnetonka, MN 55343
www.gardeningclub.com

CONTENTS

LETTER FROM THE AUTHOR

Way back in 1964, when I was 12 years old, I ran across a book unlike any I had ever seen before. It was called *Landscaping for Modern Living*, one the first books to take a new look at the home landscape and its potential. As an avid (if young) gardener, I had plenty of books which featured gardens devoted to plants. But this was the first book I had ever seen that featured gardens devoted to the needs of their owners.

Landscaping for Modern Living promoted a new concept known as "outdoor living." On page after page, its black and white photographs explored modern concepts like big patios, redwood decks, outdoor dining and cooking areas, areas set up with kids in mind, outdoor lighting and heating—in short, anything that would make an outdoor space more comfortable for human habitation.

I was bowled over. I had never thought about an outdoor space as anything other than a place to plant plants, eventually (hopefully) creating a beautiful garden. Sure there were plants in these new, outdoor living gardens, but they primarily served as attractive backdrops for human activity. And then there were those large sliding glass doors which let the outdoors into the house, and vice-versa. The whole thing was fairly revolutionary and I loved it.

It's interesting to note the slow-but-sure progress of this design revolution. With its beginnings in post World War II California, the idea spread from the West, first to the sunbelt, then through the South, eventually up the East coast, and finally throughout the Midwest. And even though today it's hard to go anywhere in this country where you don't see patios and decks and other amenities for outdoor living, it's amazing how these features continue to please and surprise their owners as something fresh and "modern." I think the revolution has endured and spread because there is something timeless and universal in the human desire to spend time outdoors in an attractive, "green," environment—an impetus decidedly different from the desire to garden.

Some stuffy types insist that a garden designed and built for outdoor living isn't really a garden at all. I disagree. It's just that in a garden designed for outdoor living the focus is on *enjoyment*, rather than work. Which doesn't mean that it can't include plenty of plants but, in the main, they will be plants that more or less take care of themselves. That doesn't make them any less beautiful; in fact, in many people's eyes, it makes them even more beautiful. And as is pointed out later in this book, one of the odd things about a garden designed for outdoor living is the fact that it may free you up to do other things—and one of those things just might be gardening! But more than likely, it will be gardening on a limited, focused basis, such as in containers or raised beds—types of gardening that don't get away from you every time you turn your back.

What makes a garden for outdoor living successful? It all boils down to one simple thing—comfort. If every decision you make concerning your landscape takes your own comfort into consideration, you'll eventually wind up with a garden you'll want to spend a lot of time in. A comfortable place to lounge with a good book on a Sunday afternoon; a shady, protected spot to serve an al fresco dinner; a convenient place to cook a meal; a safe, fun place for kids to hang out; or maybe even a spot close to your bedroom where you can take a good, hot soak—as in a hot tub or spa—on a cool, fall evening. These are all important considerations. To some, these things may seem somewhat indulgent, but I say, if you can find a way to indulge yourself and your family close to home, go ahead and indulge yourself!

In many ways, the book you hold in your hands is a direct result of that revolutionary book I held in my hands some 35 years ago. Since that time I have created many "gardens for outdoor living," both for myself and plenty of others. If this book inspires you to create your own outdoor living paradise, I'll consider it a success.

Here's to indulging in simple pleasures, close to home!

A. Cort Sinnes

CHAPTER 1

CREATING A SPACE TO LIVE OUTDOORS

Over the past two generations, there has been a significant change in the way Americans view the outdoor space surrounding their homes. Where there once was a strict division between the house and the garden, post-World War II attitudes saw an emerging desire for the pleasures of casual outdoor living. Starting in the far West, new suburban homes featured walls of glass that invited views of the outdoors in, and sliding glass doors led to decks, patios and terraces which beckoned indoor inhabitants out-of-doors. As this modern trend in home design increased in popularity, the distinction between indoors and out began to blur.

What started out as a western phenomenon has spread across the country over the last 50 years. Today, from Minnesota to Connecticut, from Oregon to Florida, homeowners, no matter where they live, want to make the most of their yards—and not just for gardens, but for people as well.

The photographs on the next seven pages explore the many pleasurable possibilities any yard offers; the hypothetical plan on page 27 combines them all into one "dream" design. Obviously, you won't include every feature presented there, but we wouldn't want you to forget anything, either!

DESIGNING & BUILDING

Once you've explored your site, examined its possibilities and come up with a plan, it's time to get busy. Whether you do the work yourself, in stages, or hire professionals to do it all at one time, it's exciting to see your dreams come to life. A word of caution: Don't be a slave to your plan. Something that looked like a great idea on paper—whether it be a curve in a patio, the height of a fence or the width of a path—may not "feel" right when it's made real and right before your eyes. As difficult as it is to tear something out and do it again differently, it's far better than looking at something, day after day, year after year, that just isn't right. Keep in mind that this is your personal space and it should be a reflection of what pleases you.

Once the "hardscape" has been installed—the fences, decks, patios, walkways and overheads have been constructed—it's time to take that long-awaited trip to the nursery or garden center. Ask anyone who's done it in reverse—namely, planted plants and then started constructing

"My own private retreat" is the way many folks talk about a garden designed with outdoor living in mind.

the hardscape—and you'll hear horror stories of how plants got trampled, covered with dirt or pulled up because they were in the

way. And remember, it's easy to be seduced by beauty at any garden center, succumbing to plants that look wonderful but are either difficult to grow or don't have a place in your yard.

If you're interested in a garden that looks lush and beautiful, but is easy to maintain, always favor plants that naturally grow well in your particular region; leave the fussy ones to people who want to baby their garden. If you're not sure what plants grow easily and well in your climate and conditions, patronize nurseries and garden centers with knowledgeable staffs. These local "experts" will quickly guide you to the plants with the most accommodating reputations.

No matter what its size, a well-designed garden makes room for any number of features, from a koi pond to outdoor dining.

As simple as it sounds, two of the most important considerations in any garden designed
for outdoor living are providing some shade
and protection from the wind.

Architectural elements, such as arbors and
pergolas, can be softened with the use of
vining plants.

PLANTING THE PLAN

As much as you may love the way a particular plant looks, make sure it's willing and able to grow in your own backyard conditions—before you make the purchase.

Gardens designed for outdoor living put the needs of people first and plants second. Which isn't to say that just because it was designed for human enjoyment, the landscape can't include elements from more traditional gardens. The trick is to concentrate the more high-maintenance types of gardening in both size and selection. If you really want an herb or rose garden, go ahead and include it in your plan, but limit it to a manageable size, select only those herbs or roses that grow willingly in your area, and make sure they're the ones least bothered by pests and diseases.

If your outdoor space is small, don't make the mistake of thinking that you can't have the plants or garden features you really want. All you have to do is scale them down in size. This holds true for water gardens—where even the smallest splashing fountain will delight both the eye and the ear—and such specialities as wildflowers, normally associated with large meadows. It's surprising how easy it is to approximate the look and feel of a field of wildflowers with a colorful planting in a raised bed next to a patio or even several large containers grouped together on a deck.

If there's one step that will make the difference between a

If there's a truism in gardening, it's this: A common plant in healthy, thriving condition, will always be more attractive than a unusual or exotic one that is barely surviving. The word "unusual" doesn't necessarily mean beautiful.

garden that almost takes care of itself and one that demands constant attention, it's advance soil preparation. Take the time to improve the soil with plenty of organic matter and other amendments, till them in properly, and you'll be amazed at how well—and fast—your plants grow. Soil preparation isn't as much fun as other aspects of gardening, but if you do it right, you'll only need to do it once, and your plants will reward your efforts for the rest of their lives.

By choosing plants whose mature size matches the space available in your yard, you'll all but eliminate the need for annual pruning.

If your schedule is a hectic one, plan your backyard with an accent on relaxing rather than gardening by keeping your plant list to a minimum.

There's nothing better than a birthday party in your own backyard: No matter what gets spilled it can be taken care of with a hose rather than a headache.

If you plan a garden for outdoor living, you can bet people will use it for just that.

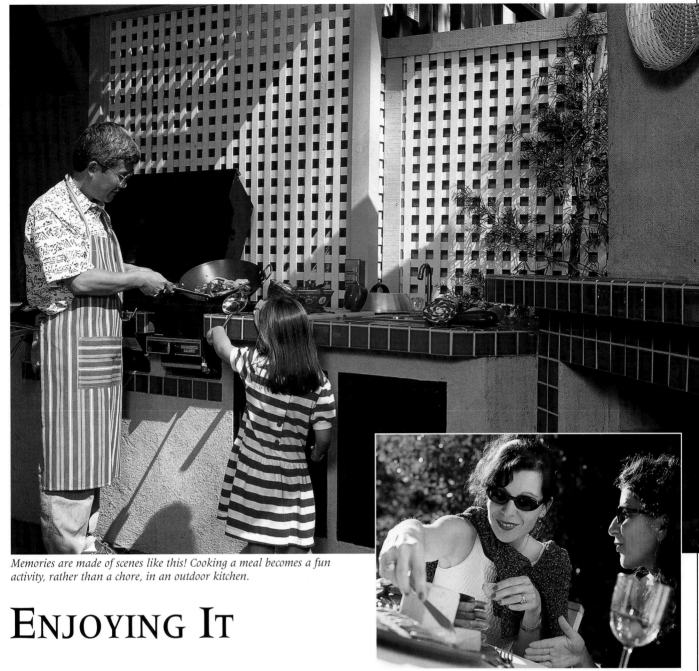

Memories are made of scenes like this! Cooking a meal becomes a fun activity, rather than a chore, in an outdoor kitchen.

A glass of wine, a wedge of cheese, a friend, and a beautiful place to enjoy it—what more could you ask for?

ENJOYING IT

I t's amazing how often people who plant traditional gardens forget to include accessories that allow the garden to be enjoyed by humans. When you set out to create a garden designed for outdoor living, items such as comfortable benches, retreats protected from the sun and wind, and places to cook and eat a meal outdoors become priorities rather than mere accessories.

For most people, outdoor living means casual and fun—not formal and stiff. A large lawn designed with outdoor games in mind, a cooking grill close to the kitchen back door, a hot tub or spa right off the master bedroom—these are all things that greatly increase the amount of pleasure your yard has to offer. While the weather is pleasant, it's not unusual for people who own a garden designed for outdoor living to spend far more time outdoors than in. After all, just about anything that can be done inside can be done outside, only more pleasantly.

If your family and friends have a particular outdoor game they like to play, whether it's horseshoes, croquet or badminton, be sure to find out the dimensions of a regulation field of play and plan your lawn accordingly. It may seem rather frivolous to plan a lawn based on the dimensions of a volleyball court, but then what's so frivolous about having close-to-home fun with your family and friends?

THE PLANNING PROCESS

A beautiful spring morning dawns and you find yourself taking a hard look at your backyard—for the first time in a long time. What you see is not a pretty sight. Overcome by enthusiasm and the need to do something—anything—to improve your yard, you simply start in without any plan whatsoever: mowing an overgrown lawn, hacking away at some brutish weeds, and, finally, as a reward, taking a trip to the local nursery or garden center. Once you're home and the plants that caught your eye in the nursery are firmly in the ground, you're probably not quite sure what you've done, but there's some contentment with the fact that at least you've done something.

Working without a plan is risky business on two counts. First, plants you purchased on impulse rarely wind up in a location that's best for them. Second, if you're interested in a yard as a living space for people, plants are among the last things you add.

If this scenario sounds familiar, you're not alone. When it comes to creating a "landscape," the most common mistake people make is confusing the planting process with the process of creating an outdoor living space for people. Although plants definitely help, they are only one component in creating a satisfying landscape for living. Without a plan, one spontaneous spurt of action usually follows another, right up to the almost inevitable, unsatisfactory conclusion: an outdoor space that satisfies neither plants nor people.

Plan or no plan? Only you can answer the question. Reading the following pages can help you develop clear ideas of what you want your yard to provide and how you want it to look—specifically. This will lead to a plan on paper, which will help you, or someone you hire, make sure those ideas take shape in reality.

Having a plan will help you create a beautiful, usable outdoor living space.

For those of you who haven't done a thing yet except sit and look at your yard, you've already done the best thing you can do to get started. The next step is to get up off the stoop and walk around—but that's getting ahead of the story. Before walking around your yard, walk backward—through time—to find a few of the things that could be important in creating your own personal outdoor retreat.

There's a lot to be said for taking your time with the planning process: You can change your mind as many times as you like, with very little expenditure of time, money or effort. The motto is: Plan now, plant later.

Above: Indulge yourself! Many people consider—and rightly so—that no yard for outdoor living is complete without a hammock.

Left: There are few things more appealing than sitting outdoors on a cool night with your feet propped up against a blazing fire—right in your own backyard.

Most backyards have plenty of room for a small outbuilding perfect for use as an artist's studio, hideaway or, if you must, tool storage.

DETERMINING YOUR OWN STYLE

You undoubtedly remember an outdoor place, either real or imagined, that deeply satisfied you as a child or young adult. It may have been an elderly neighbor's flower garden, with dahlias as big as your head, 3-foot-tall marigolds and trailing nasturtiums that nearly covered the pathways. Or it may have been farther afield, like that shady, cool grove of pine trees where cookouts were held at summer camp. Perhaps it was your uncle's vegetable garden, where you

had your first taste of a warm, sun-ripened tomato right off the vine (made so much more intriguing when that tiny shaker of salt appeared like magic from behind a stone bench). Or maybe it was that fort you made from scrap lumber, which seemed like the neatest place in the world because it was yours, built out of your imagination and with your own two hands.

Any yard holds the potential to satisfy you in the same way as any of those early outdoor experiences.

The first step in creating a satisfying place, however, is to identify, as clearly as you can, what it was that appealed to you. Pull a lounge chair out onto the porch or under a shady tree and ask yourself: What was it about that old neighbor's flower garden that made it so compelling? Was it a jumble of plants, one tumbling over the other, an almost wild scene of color and fragrance, like walking into a domestic jungle—perhaps just the opposite of your parents' tidy yard? What made

Want to re-create the feeling of a mountain lake in your backyard? Why not! You really can do it, and it's probably not as expensive as you might think.

It's your backyard and you can do whatever you like with it— even if it means turning your space into an outdoor model railroad extravaganza.

that fort so great? The feeling of enclosure, of being able to see out but not be seen? Or the fact that everything you needed for comfort and protection was close at hand? And that vegetable garden—was it simply that the food was growing right before your eyes that made it so attractive? Or was it the sensual delight of being able to bite right into a tomato and let the juice run down your face and bare tummy, without being told it wasn't a proper thing to do?

You don't need to write down these thoughts and feelings, but bear them in mind throughout each stage of the following design process. Trust your instincts and be willing to modify your plan, even if the only reason you can give for doing so is because "it just doesn't feel right." In the pragmatic world of committing plans to paper, the list of instructions rarely includes "follow your heart." But when it comes to creating a satisfying garden for the best in outdoor living,

perhaps it should be added, right up there near the top.

One last thing: Keep in mind Thomas Wolfe's caveat; namely, that "you can't go home again." Of course, he was right. You can't. The point of digging in the past is not to duplicate exactly some childhood memory, but to identify the way those places made you feel. It's no accident that the most satisfying gardens are born from a childlike imagination and an adult, devil-may-care vitality.

GETTING STARTED

At this stage in planning a garden for outdoor living, it's time to move from the past to the present. Here are the supplies you'll need to assemble: a binder, approximately 200 sheets of binder paper, scissors, several sharp pencils with good erasers, tape, ruler and a few sheets of standard graph paper.

ery, hardware store or lumberyard, and it will help you avoid disappointments when you deal with contractors, carpenters, bricklayers, concrete masons and landscapers.

If you take the time to create a binder filled with the details of what you like in a garden, you'll go a long way in answering specific questions. For instance, instead of

fense, contractors and tradespeople are put in a difficult position when they are expected to make real what they think is in the client's mind. So do everyone a favor: assemble your own garden scrapbook before the first shovelful of earth is turned.

Pick a quiet time to go through the magazines, and look at them slowly and deliberately. Carefully search the corners of each photograph to see if anything catches your eye. It might be something as simple as the handle on a gate, a piece of outdoor furniture, the shape of a deck or the color of an awning. No detail is insignificant when it comes to designing your own outdoor haven.

Each time you see something appealing in a photograph or illustration, cut the picture out of the magazine and tape it to a piece of binder paper. Be sure to make notations on the paper as to what it is, specifically, that you like. Without notes, three months later, in an entirely different frame of mind, you may find yourself wondering what it was in the photograph that caught your eye.

At this stage, you don't really need to organize the scrapbook. It's enough just to make sure that the pages get put into the binder so they won't get scattered to the

Dreaming about your ideal yard can be a relaxing and rewarding process. Consult as many books and magazines as you can—the results will be worth it.

With these materials—combined with an armful of home and garden magazines—the object is to create your own personal garden design scrapbook. This may sound rather sophomoric, but it's the best thing you can do to ensure that your garden turns out the way you want it to be. The scrapbook will be invaluable on trips to the nurs-

waving your hands in the air and hoping for the best, you can use your binder of images to point out exactly what you want: "I want this pattern picket for the fence, with this type of finial on the posts, the whole thing painted white, with a gate exactly like this, with this—right here—this set of hinges and that type of latch." In their de-

winds. There will be plenty of time to organize the images later.

Depending on your sense of urgency, you can assemble the scrapbook over a long weekend, over a few months or slowly over a period of years. This process benefits from a leisurely approach, allowing for changes in needs, tastes and desires. If, however, you have a specific deadline or timetable—like "this is the year we're going to fix up the backyard, and we're going to finish it before Labor Day"—look at as many magazines as you can get your hands on to see the widest possible range of ideas.

Bear in mind that, during this stage, anything is possible, as you are literally creating your "dream" garden. Further into the planning process you may find out that the flagstone patio you admired in a particular photograph is simply too expensive or that the jasmine that covered a trellis in another won't grow in your climate. Take heart in knowing that you'll almost always find a suitable substitute that supplies the same look and feel you find so attractive. Right now, as you create your imaginary outdoor living space, allow yourself free rein in selecting all those items and features that catch your eye. If you start constraining your vision now, you may never achieve the garden of your dreams. There will be plenty of time for practicalities, substitutions and compromises later, but at least they'll all conform to the overall idea and "look" of what you want to achieve.

A Word about Plants

Whether you already know some of the plants you want in your garden or are completely new to gardening, coming up with the plant list for your particular project takes some time and effort. The process is outlined on pages 80-105 and, if you're interested in creating a garden meant for enjoyment rather than work, you'll be wise to consider the advice carefully. In a garden designed for outdoor living, the plants serve as a backdrop for human activity. That doesn't mean that the backdrop can't be beautiful—it most certainly can—but to keep your garden from becoming a high-maintenance series of demands, you'll want to choose your plants carefully.

For some, the ideal outdoor living space is one that can be neatly manicured with a minimum of fuss.

The type of outdoor living garden you create will not only reflect your taste, but the amount of time you have to actually spend tending plants.

GETTING TO KNOW YOUR YARD

To make the most of its potential, you need to know every corner of your yard intimately. You may think you know it already, but you'd be surprised at how many people are locked into only one viewing position, usually about 6 feet away from the back door! Get acquainted with your yard by walking its perimeter all the way to the edges of the property. While you walk, keep looking back at your house. Is there a spot, somewhere toward the rear or to the side of the yard, where the view of your house is particularly pleasant? Would this be the best place for a small, free-standing deck or patio, just right for a couple of chairs and a couple of cool ones as evening shadows lengthen? Or is there a spot beneath a group of mature trees at the back of the yard that you discover to be delightfully shady? Conventional wisdom has it that outdoor eating areas should be located as close to the house as possible, but a big picnic table under that far-off leafy canopy just might be the nicest place to enjoy a meal. It's worth considering.

And is that the perfect, almost horizontal, limb on which to hang a swing? How about the area behind the shrubbery and under a tree, in the far corner of your lot ... do you feel a sense of security and diminished scale that reminds you of places you liked to play in as a child? Perhaps this is the spot for a small secret garden for the kids in your house, or for those who

regularly visit your yard. All that's necessary is a layer of fine bark, perhaps a couple of sawed-off logs to use as table and chairs, a kid's imagination and a playful adult to lead the way.

During this stage of the game, the point is to make the most out of what you have and to make

As you get to know your yard on better terms, hopefully you'll run across the perfect spot to hang a hammock.

sure you are not overlooking any possibilities. While it pays to take an imaginative approach to your yard, there are certain practicalities you'll want to take into consideration. Is there a prevailing wind you'll want to block to make an outdoor dining spot more comfortable? Are there trees that need to be pruned to allow enough sunlight to support a lawn? What about views? Any that you'd like to block with a screen of some kind—or a desirable view that can only be seen if a mature tree is removed? Perhaps that low spot in your yard that always seems to collect moisture is the best place for a pond, or a dry, rocky upslope the perfect spot for a wildflower planting that's content with a minimum of attention.

As you walk around your yard, you may start to have new ideas about where some of the elements you want should go. This is the easiest (not to mention the least expensive) time to change your mind—repeatedly, if desired. And even though implementing these ideas may not be in your immediate future, it's important to take into consideration all the elements of your dream garden. This is the only way to make sure there's room for everything, that the various elements come together in a harmonious way—and that you don't end up building a concrete patio where you might eventually want to dig a hole for a goldfish pond.

Above: Sometimes a problem can be turned into asset. Here a low, rocky spot in this landscape turned out to be the perfect spot for an elevated, covered deck that is connected to the rest of the yard with a boardwalk.

Left: Here's another solution for a low spot. If it's going to collect water anyway, why not turn it into a pond? That's what these owners did, much to their satisfaction and delight.

THREE-DIMENSIONAL THINKING

The next step is to take your backyard scrapbook to the yard, along with a few dozen 12-inch wooden stakes, a half-dozen 2-inch by 2-inch by 6-foot wooden stakes (available at any lumberyard), a spool of heavy cotton string or twine (500 feet should do), a couple of long garden hoses, two handfuls of clothespins and a few old bed sheets. An odd list of equipment, to be sure, but it works.

Put your equipment aside for a moment, and take a good look at your scrapbook. What have you got? You may have some ideas for fences, a play area for the kids, a deck or patio, perhaps a gazebo or an arbor, a really great tree house, an outside eating and cooking area, an expanse of grass laid out with lawn games in mind, or even a fountain, swimming pool or spa. Your challenge is to arrange the elements you want in the space available.

Any square- or rectangle-shaped feature (such as a deck, patio, swimming pool or sandbox) can be outlined using the stakes and string. Simply pound the stakes a few inches into the ground, and tie the string around the stakes to show the outline. Curved areas, such as lawns and planting beds, are easily outlined using a long garden hose (or several hoses connected together). Adjust the curves in the hose until the shape is pleasing from all angles, including from the window inside the house where it will most often be viewed.

To a person with little or no involvement in your design process, this mocked-up landscape plan may appear a motley mess. Where someone else sees only a sheet hanging from a line, you see a brick and lattice-work fence. That garden hose, lying in a curve on the ground, isn't just lying there; it's marking the boundaries of a lush green lawn. And with the help of a little more imagination, those four stakes over there in the shade of the tree are easily transformed into a sandbox where a child contentedly plays. The best part of this exercise is the three-dimensional quality it gives your emerging plan, something almost impossible to achieve with only pencil and paper, which happens to be the next step.

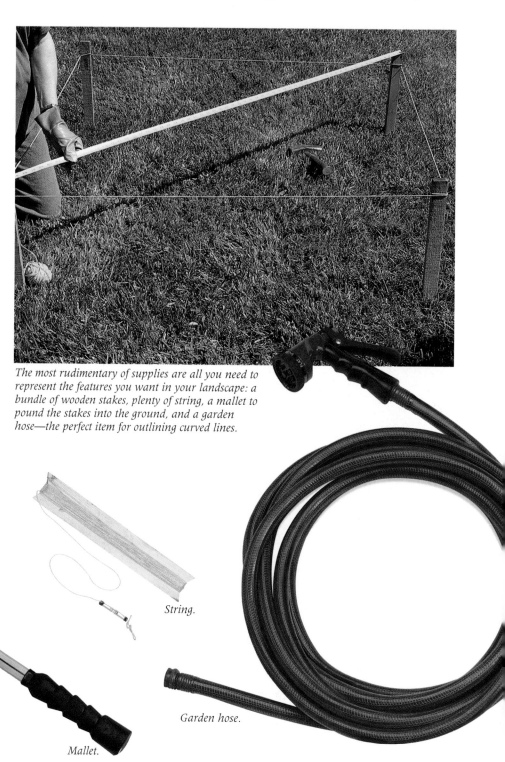

The most rudimentary of supplies are all you need to represent the features you want in your landscape: a bundle of wooden stakes, plenty of string, a mallet to pound the stakes into the ground, and a garden hose—the perfect item for outlining curved lines.

String.

Garden hose.

Mallet.

Watching your plan-on-paper turn into an abstract design outlined with stakes, strings and a garden hose—and then finally evolve into the real thing—is an extremely satisfying process every step of the way.

COMMITTING THE THREE-DIMENSIONAL PLAN TO PAPER

Once you've collected your early memories and your present-day, "three-dimensional" ideas, it's time to make use of some graph paper—as long as you heed a couple of important warnings.

The most creative people in the world can become absolute robots when faced with a sheet of graph paper. Just because there are little blue squares all over the page in a perfect grid pattern doesn't mean you aren't allowed to draw a curve, or draw a line in between two of the printed lines. Remember, *you* are the one determining the plans, not the graph paper.

While virtually every book ever written on the subject of home landscaping stresses the importance of committing a plan to paper, the abstract and precise nature of the process presents some hazards to creativity. Yes, it is important for you to know the dimensions of the lot, which direction the prevailing winds blow, what the exposure of the yard is (morning or afternoon sun or shade), the location of water spigots, electrical outlets, and so forth. But there's something seductive in putting these hard-and-fast facts down on paper that makes it possible to design the life and spirit right out of the project.

Leave the stakes, sheets and hoses in place for a couple of days, or weeks if necessary. See how the arrangement looks at different times of the day and in different weather conditions. Once you're comfortable with the layout, get out the tape measure, pencils and paper.

Make a rough drawing of the shape of your lot and house—and please note the word *rough*. Even those who feel that they simply can't draw anything should go ahead and rough in this preliminary drawing, because it has to make sense to only one person—you—at this point. Use this rough plan to note the actual measurements.

A well-planned and executed landscape is evident from the moment you first enter it.

CREATING THE PLAN

To start creating your plan, you'll have to place the existing features of your property—house, driveway, sidewalks, trees and terrain features. To begin, measure the outside perimeter of your lot.

Then measure in from the lot lines to the outside walls of your house to establish the house's position on the lot.

Finally, measure the outlines of your intended deck, patio, play area, pool, sandbox or whatever it is you're considering. To correctly position everything on the plan, you'll need to measure in from the lot line, just as you did with your house.

And, yes, now is the time to indicate the location of water spigots, electrical outlets and whatever else you think should be taken into consideration.

Once you have the measurements on the rough plan, transfer them to the graph paper and make a nice, tidy drawing—one that you can show with pride to any landscaper, architect or contractor. Alternately, if you doubt your ability to draw, ask someone who can draw to do it for you, with you sitting there explaining what all of those strange lines and squiggles mean. If a single sheet of graph paper is too confining, tape several sheets together to make a bigger drawing.

By the time you have the finished plan on paper, you should be confident that you have a design based in reality rather than an abstract, two-dimensional drawing pulled together on your kitchen table. This, combined with your garden scrapbook, will stand you in good stead as you go about making your plans and dreams come to life.

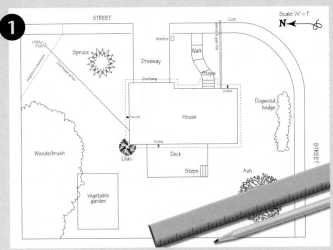

1. Make measurements and draw out your property and its "permanent" features.

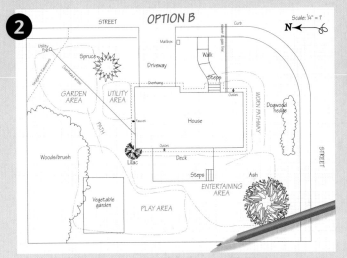

2. Add the general location, shape and size of the kinds of areas you're thinking of—play spots, pathways, garden beds, entertaining areas, etc.

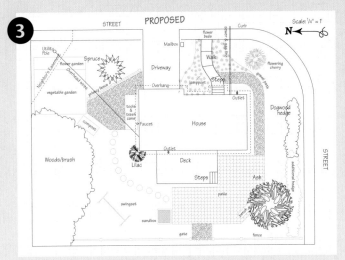

3. Fine-tune the plan after plenty of consideration, coming down to precise indications of what goes where.

DO-IT-YOURSELF OR CONTRACT IT?

Now's the time for you to face another kind of reality—the fiscal kind. Putting cost estimates together can be a very time-consuming job, and you may decide to leave it to a professional. This, of course, depends on whether you intend to do the work yourself or hire someone else to do it for you.

Although this is largely a personal decision, it should be pointed out that most yard construction (with the exception of pools, spas, fountains and sophisticated electrical work) is well within the ability of a person with average mechanical aptitude. If you enjoy these kinds of projects, by all means, have at it; you'll save considerable labor charges and experience a great deal of pride once the project is completed.

If, however, you decide you have neither the time nor the inclination to do the work yourself, a variety of professionals and semiprofessionals are available. The type of help you

Installing the hardscape in any yard requires basic construction skills, such as knowing how to use a level.

choose depends both on the complexity of your plans and on any personal contacts you have in the field. You may be better off using someone with whom you have a relationship that goes beyond a mere contract. The vagaries of contracting any type of work to a person completely unknown to you are well documented. An already

If you're in doubt about your ability to perform the skills and labor needed to do a job safely and correctly, you'll be better off hiring professionals to do the work.

established personal relationship with any contractor could be your best insurance for the successful completion of your project.

You have many choices for outside help. They are presented here in traditional order of "professionalism" (that is, from the least to most amount of training and licensing required to use the title): nursery or garden center design/construction service, landscape designer, landscape contractor and landscape architect. On the straight construction side (in the same order), there are handy people, carpenters, building designers, building contractors and architects. Some of these titles may differ from one part of the country to the other, but, regardless of the title, you'll be able to find someone at each level of skill no matter where you live.

Some people claim that you're always better off using only the top professionals in the field. This is certainly true with large and complex projects. But if your project is of small or moderate size, it's possible to get excellent results from general handy people, retirees with extra time on their hands and all manner of artists and crafts people who are looking to augment their income.

Be forewarned that this will not be the type of working relationship where you can go away for a 2-week vacation and expect the project to be finished upon your return. Any time construction is in progress, someone will need to be on hand to answer questions, to respond to suggested changes in the plans and to make sure that the work is, in fact, proceeding in a timely manner.

Once the construction of your new backyard actually begins, an odd thing happens. As soon as the first section of fence is hammered into place, or your future lawn starts to fill in with the delicate shades of new blades of grass, your imagination takes over and completes the project in your mind's eye. That's why ground-breaking ceremonies attract so much attention. A project that you may have discussed for years is finally on the way to becoming reality. You may not be erecting a 40-story skyscraper,

Masonry walls and complex, multi-level walkways are probably best left to professionals.

One of the benefits of hiring a professional contractor is their knowledge of newer construction techniques, such as these molded concrete pavers used to form a rustic-looking walkway.

but as the creator of your own garden for outdoor living, you'll experience plenty of excitement as you take the first concrete steps beyond those vaporous ideas and paper plans. Here's to your own private ground-breaking ceremony!

DO-IT-YOURSELF ADVICE

Trying to decide whether to tackle a construction project yourself, or hire it done? Here are the pros and cons of doing a project yourself:

Pros: 1) you'll save money, 2) gain personal satisfaction and a sense of accomplishment (not to mention the possible learning of new skills) and 3) the final results will be a direct interpretation of your vision and talent.

Cons: 1) the project will probably take longer if you do it yourself (in fact, many do-it-yourself projects never get finished), 2) the final results may not be as professional as if you had hired it done, 3) you may run into unforeseen and expensive problems and 4) it can be a lot of hard physical work.

Not all do-it-yourself projects are created equal. A homeowner with moderate construction skills will find any project that uses small construction units the easiest to handle. For example, a brick patio laid over a sand base can be constructed one small section at a time; a concrete patio, on the other hand, usually requires that all the concrete be poured at one time, requiring considerable speed and skill on the part of the person installing it. A wooden fence, constructed in a straight line, is well within the scope of most do-it-yourselfers, but a multi-level deck with stairs may prove unrealistic and downright frustrating for anyone less than a professional carpenter. A small garden pond, using a preformed fiberglass or plastic liner (or one made from the new butyl rubber sold by the yard) is relatively painless to install (with the exception of digging the hole), while a traditional concrete-lined pond or pool challenges the abilities of most backyard do-it-yourselfers.

In general, any project governed by local building codes and ordinances, such as electrical installations, plumbing and engineered drainage systems, are best left to the pros.

Some projects, such as this elevated deck, practically demand the advanced engineering and carpentry skills possessed by professionals.

For all their charm, picket fences are simple enough to be built by homeowners with only the most basic of carpentry skills.

Some garden pools, such as this geometric one with tilework back-walls, employ more sophisticated construction techniques that are best left to professionals.

With the advent of rigid plastic pond liners, the hardest part about creating a simple garden pond is digging the hole!

WHAT'S IN A NAME?

When you start looking for some professional help in either the design or construction of your yard, the first place you might look is in the yellow pages. You may not think of your yard as a landscape, but that's probably where you'll find the kind of help you're looking for—under the heading "Landscape." Listings include landscape architects, landscape contractors and landscape designers.

Although it's difficult to gauge the merits of one individual or firm against the merits of another based on the information in the yellow pages, it's a good place to start. Just don't expect to find the service you need with the first call; treat this like an interviewing process.

If the landscape service expresses an interest in your project (after you've described the type of help you need, the approximate size of your yard and the size of your budget), it's time for you to ask some questions (see sidebar "questions to ask a landscape pro").

QUESTIONS TO ASK A LANDSCAPE PRO

1 How long have you been in business?

2 Do you specialize in a certain type of work?

3 What type of contract do you offer?

4 Where could I go to see some examples of your work?

5 Could you provide a reference list of previous clients I could call?

Many hands make for fast work: You can just about guarantee that a professional landscape construction crew will be able to finish your job in a fraction of the time it would take you.

The pros know that a good edging, installed between a lawn and an adjoining planting bed, will save any homeowner much time and energy.

Be sure to take notes, and keep them in a file or in your garden scrapbook, for future reference.

If the firm or individuals you talk with determine that their talents are not suited to your needs, be sure to ask them for other recommendations. And once you find someone who fits the bill, don't stop there. It's surprising how much you can learn about the field simply by talking with a half-dozen or so people.

After you decide on a particular person or firm, check with the contractor's state license board. Verify the contractor's license, and see if the company is bonded and carries insurance for workers' compensation. This simple procedure can save you many headaches. For information regarding a contractor's performance and reliability, contact the Better Business Bureau.

If you're satisfied with your findings, the next step is to enter into a contract. Although contracts vary, certain basics always apply. Any written contract should include the following:

ELEMENTS OF A GOOD CONTRACT

1 An approximate date to start installation or construction.

2 A completion date.

3 What happens if the project is not completed on time.

4 Specifications for all materials and equipment (including plants).

5 Guarantees and warranties for specified equipment (such as lighting systems, irrigation systems and so on).

6 A schedule of payments, with the last and quite significant payment tied to the completion of the project, or, better, slightly after.

Above and left: One way or another, any landscape features which need to be level—such as patios, terraces and walkways—will need to go through the "leveling" process, either by hand and shovel or with larger pieces of equipment. This is an important step, often overlooked by do-it-yourselfers.

CHAPTER 2

"STICKS & STONES"

When you start thinking about your outdoor space as space to live in, not just to garden in, a shift in priorities occurs. Where you once saw places for flower beds, shrub borders and a vegetable garden, you now see the need for places where human activities can take place comfortably. Which is not to say that a yard planned for outdoor living won't have room for flower beds, shrub borders and a vegetable garden; it very well may. It's just that those features will take up less space, leaving more room for living outdoors and enjoying it.

Concrete is probably the most popular material for home patios, and for good reason: It is relatively inexpensive, can achieve any shape or form, and is extremely long-lasting.

PATIOS & TERRACES

Your first priority in designing a garden with outdoor living in mind may be as simple as finding a spot where you can sit and enjoy the great out-of-doors. That spot can be, as you wish, either warm and sunny, or cool and shady (or a place with opportunities for both), but not so breezy that the newspaper or tablecloth blows away. The spot may also provide some degree of privacy and perhaps some overhead protection from a sudden shower or the midday sun. Besides something to sit on, which is discussed in Chapter 5 (pages 106-119), the most important factor in creating a comfortable place to sit outdoors is a flat, stable surface for those fundamental pieces of furniture—chairs and a table.

Choices for creating that flat, stable surface for outdoor living run the gamut from patios and terraces to wooden decks and porches, all of which are usually connected directly to the house itself. If the most comfortable and inviting place to sit is farther afield, say at the far corner of your yard, you might want to consider a freestanding garden patio or deck.

What's the difference between a patio and a terrace? The concept of a terrace is often associated with a view, which means that most traditional terraces sit on a slightly higher level than the surrounding ground. The origins of the word patio contain the opposite concept, namely, that of an enclosed outdoor space.

If, when you hear the word "patio," you think of the far West and Southwest regions of the United States, you're right to do so. The fact that the word itself is Spanish tells us a lot, because it was the Spanish missionaries who imported the concept of a patio to the New World back in the 18th and 19th centuries—a concept Webster's dictionary defines as "a courtyard; especially an inner court open to the sky." If you've had the opportunity to visit any of the surviving missions in the far West, you probably returned with images of the lushly planted patio courtyards so typical of this type of architecture.

Enclosed or open, with a view or not, a patio or terrace still serves the same purpose: providing a readily accessible place to enjoy the outdoors, with some of the comforts of indoors. Some things have changed, however. Where early Spanish missionaries had few choices for building materials (the floors of most early patios were simply packed earth), homeowners today face a dizzying array of choices. Pictured on the following pages is a gallery of outdoor flooring choices with a brief description of their characteristics.

It's hard to find fault with a traditional brick patio—here, the bricks are set in concrete—simply for the effortless and lovely way it blends into a garden setting.

Here, a classic, narrow terrace offers the perfect opportunity to step out of the house and admire the view below.

All the indoor comforts, outdoors: Table, chairs, sofa, all comfortably arranged on a warm tile patio. Outdoor living at its best!

BRICK PATIOS

The warm red color of bricks makes a wonderful complement to garden greenery. It's a classic combination which never goes out of style.

A brick patio is a good project for a beginning do-it-yourselfer, because the work can be done in manageable stages. Bricks come in many textures and colors. The two most popular bricks for patios and terraces are smooth-surface face bricks and the more porous common bricks. Used bricks make an attractive surface but must be chosen carefully since the rough surfaces of some may be hard on bare feet. Because a load of bricks is so heavy, have them delivered and stacked as near to the project as possible. When estimating quantity, plan to use five bricks per square foot, which allows for extras lost to breakage.

The most common method of installation is to place bricks on a level bed of sand at least 1 inch thick. For more solid or permanent patios, bricks are laid on a bed of concrete mortar, although the sand method is more than adequate for

Irregular bricks simply laid on a bed of sand, for an informal look.

Bricks laid in the traditional "herringbone" pattern, mortared into place.

This unusual brick pattern leaves regular spaces for groundcover plantings.

An interesting combination: landscape timbers in a repeating pattern between bricks.

most purposes. A brick patio should slope *slightly* away from the house to allow for surface drainage. And when planting around (or in) a brick patio, select plants whose root systems won't dislodge the bricks.

To begin with, make it easier on yourself by designing a patio that fits the dimensions of the bricks that you are using, taking into consideration the standard 1/4-inch space between each brick. This simple step will save many hours of tedious brick cutting. Most bricks for outdoor construction projects are labeled SW (severe weathering), MW (moderate weathering), NW (no weathering). Where winters include freezing temperatures, use SW grade bricks; in milder, frost-free climates, MW grade bricks. NW bricks should not be used for outdoor construction projects no matter where you live.

If you do need to cut bricks, ask at your local hardware store for a wide brick chisel (sometimes called a bolster). The best tool for using with this chisel is a ball peen hammer. Always wear safety glasses when cutting brick.

How to Install a Brick Patio

1 Using string and stakes, mark the outline of your brick patio.

2 Excavate the soil to a depth of 4$^1/4$ inches (based on a 2-inch layer of sand and a 2 $^1/4$-inch depth of common brick).

3 Level the surface of the excavation, with a *slight* grade away from the house to allow for water drainage.

4 Spray the excavated area with a preemergent weed killer.

5 Pour sand to a depth of 2 inches. Level bed with rake and spray bed lightly with water to compact it.

6 Begin laying bricks in pattern of your choice (see photo examples on this page) using $^1/4$-inch-thick spacers (a small square of cardboard will do the trick), and use a level to make sure the bricks are even as you go along.

7 Once the bricks have been laid, sprinkle dry sand to fill in cracks, sweeping it into place.

8 As a last step, sprinkle brick surface with a fine jet of water to settle sand and to clean the surface of your new patio.

Goggles.

Bolster.

Ball peen hammer.

The tools needed for cutting bricks are few. The essentials include a pair of goggles, a bolster for the actual cutting, and a ball peen hammer.

CONCRETE PATIOS

Concrete is an amazingly versatile construction material, readily accepting a wide variety of finishes (such as this stained version) and imprinted patterns.

Wooden forms, which will ultimately be removed, hold the concrete in place while it cures.

Concrete is a mixture of cement, sand and gravel. Concrete patios can be made in virtually any shape or size, with a variety of surface textures from smooth to rough, depending on how the surface is finished. With the popular exposed aggregate finish, gravel in the concrete is exposed by washing away the finer cement particles. Exposed aggregate is more natural-looking than smooth-finish concrete; it also provides a low-glare surface.

Small concrete patios and walkways can be owner-built. For a small project, use dry-mixed concrete, which comes in 90-pound sacks; all you add is the water and muscle. For a larger surface, it's advisable to have ready-mixed concrete delivered and poured in place. Make sure the site is accessible to a large truck. You can do the finish work yourself, or hire a masonry contractor.

Concrete patios require wood forms to hold the concrete in place until it sets. Forms for curving patios are made from thin, flexible boards. Make sure to have all the forms built prior to ordering or buying concrete.

If you're planning on installing a concrete patio yourself, realize that the project must be carefully choreographed from start to finish. Have an outline of the patio completely formed, using sturdy 2 by 4's and stakes. Form curves using 3 or 4 layers of bender board (available at your local lumberyard) and as many stakes as you need to hold the curve in place. In addition to the form, make sure your helpers are on time and that you have all your tools at hand. In addition to regular carpentry and garden tools (such as hammers, shovels, rakes and the like), have the following special concrete tools, shown on these pages available: a tamper, a darby or bull float, an edging trowel, a joiner and a rectangular concrete trowel.

Concrete tamper.

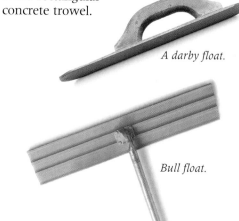

A darby float.

Bull float.

For a nonslip, nonglare surface, request an exposed aggregate finish on your concrete patio.

A hand-held groove tool for applying control grooves on wet concrete to control cracking.

A hand-held edger gently rounds the edges of a concrete slab, making them less prone to chipping.

Concrete edgers also come with long handles to make the edging job easier on your back.

HOW TO INSTALL A CONCRETE PATIO

1   Make the outline of your patio, using stakes and string.

2   Excavate the soil to a depth of 4 inches.

3   Using the tamper, compact the excavated surface.

4   Spray the surface with a preemergent weed killer.

5   Using 2 by 4's or bender board, form the outline of the patio: tops of the forms should be 1 inch above soil level.

6   Pound stakes on the outside of the form, and nail securely.

7   Add a 1-inch layer of pea gravel or crushed rock.

8   Roll out wire reinforcing mesh over the gravel bed; cut to fit inside forms. Slip rocks underneath mesh to hold it, about halfway up the side of the form.

9   Give the signal to pour the concrete.

10 Use a 2 by 4 long enough to extend beyond the sides of the edges of the form to begin leveling or "striking the concrete." Two people are needed for this step. Hold the 2 by 4 firmly against the top of the form, and drag across the newly poured concrete to level it. Jiggle the 2 by 4 back and forth in a sawing motion as you go; several passes may be necessary.

11 After the concrete has been poured and striked, use the bull or darby floats to further smooth the concrete, pushing the aggregate to beneath the surface.

12 Use the edger float around the perimeter of the form to compact and round the edge of the patio (this helps keep the edges of the patio from chipping).

13 Add control joints to prevent cracking. Use the jointer for this process, with a straight board as a guide. Use nails (not hammered all the way in) to temporarily secure guide board to form. Add parallel control grooves every 5 or 6 feet; patios wider than 10 feet should include a control groove perpendicular.

14 Use the concrete trowel for the final smoothing step. (Note: For large patios it is advisable to have more than one person troweling.)

15 To cure concrete, cover the slab with plastic sheeting held loosely in place with 2 by 4's. Keep in place for at least a week to allow concrete to bond properly.

Concrete is one of the few landscape construction materials which can be readily shaped into virtually any curved shape.

PAVING STONES & PEA GRAVEL

Paving stones run the gamut from small pebbles to flagstones to precast concrete "cobblestones." Any type of paving stone can be set in concrete, mortar or sand. Each type of paving stone has a distinct look, and prices range from expensive (flagstone) to inexpensive (pea gravel).

Pea gravel is a rustic option that is a favorite throughout the European countryside, where a gravel patio is often complemented by an arbor overhead, covered with a venerable grape vine. The type of pea gravel available will depend, somewhat, on where you live. Because of its great weight,

pea gravel is mined locally and usually not shipped more than 100 miles or so from its source.

The first step in creating a pea gravel "patio" is to completely remove any weeds from the area. You can spray the area with a preemergent weed killer, but it's not completely necessary because

Almost every geographic region in the country produces some type of native stone slabs for use in landscape projects. The effect is a rugged one, built to last a lifetime or two.

a 2-inch layer of gravel does a surprisingly good job of deterring the germination of any weed seeds. Do not apply more than a 2-inch layer of pea gravel; any deeper than that and it becomes unstable for chairs and people to stand on. Pea gravel is very inexpensive, and once you wheelbarrow and rake it into place, you're done. Spilled drinks disappear in an instant without leaving stains, leaves rake up or blow away easily and the gravel has a pleasant crunch underfoot.

Laying paving stone is similar to the process for laying out a brick patio on page 38. Note, however, that there are two types of stone available for use in patios, terraces and walkways: precut or dress stone, and uncut or irregular stone (sometimes called flagstone). One of the keys to success with either precut or irregular stones is to do a "dry run" before actually setting the stones in your patio. This way you can take your time making sure the stones create a pleasing, even pattern and that you have, in fact, enough stones to complete the project.

To lay precut or dress stone, follow the instructions for a concrete patio on page 40, but note that the slab need only be 2 or 3 inches thick, and there is no need to worry about the finish of its surface, as you will be covering it with the stone. Also, the slab need cure for only 24 hours before proceeding with the laying of the stone. Mix premixed mortar according to the instructions on the sack, and apply

Although they are hard to find, cobblestones create an old-world effect for patios and walkways.

Any paving stone, whether cut or irregular, can be permanently held in place using mortar.

over the concrete slab about 1 inch thick about the size of two or three stones. Place the stones on top of the mortar leaving about 1/2 inch between them. Tap the stones into the mortar gently, using a rubber mallet; with each small section you install, check using a level, and make any adjustments quickly before the mortar has a chance to set. Repeat this process two or three stones at a time, until the patio is

complete. Joints between stones should be level with the stones themselves. If necessary, mix additional mortar and trowel into place, wiping off excess mortar with a damp rag.

If you are creating a patio walkway or terrace with flagstone or irregular cut stones, it is doubly important to lay out the pattern ahead of time. When setting stones into the bed of sand, leave a space of about 1/2 inch between the stones. Most irregular stone has a relatively flat side, and one that can be quite bumpy. The flat side is the side you want on top, so you may have to do a little excavating of the sand to accommodate the stone's bumpy side. After you complete each small section, use a level and adjust as necessary. After all the stones are laid, spread a layer of sand over the patio, and sweep to fill in the joints between the stones. Spray with a fine jet of water to further compact the sand. You may have to repeat this process one or two more times to completely fill in the joints.

If you decide to go with some sort of crushed rock (left) or pea gravel (right), you're best off going directly to the supplier to make your choice, which will range greatly in texture, size and color.

TILE PATIOS

Like paving stones, there are many types of tile available for outdoor patio use, from irregular, low-fired Mexican tiles to high-fired, highly uniform terra-cotta tiles. Choose unglazed tiles for outdoor use because their relatively nonslip surface makes for greater safety. Glazed tiles may be too slick (especially when wet) to walk on safely. Tiles can be laid over concrete or level, compacted sand. On concrete, tiles are permanently mortared into position with joints from 1/4 to 1/2 inch wide.

To lay ceramic or quarry tiles, follow the instructions for a concrete patio on pages 40-41, but note that the slab need only be 2 or 3 inches thick, and there is no need to worry about the finish of its surface, as you will be covering it with the tile. Also, the slab need cure for only 24 hours before proceeding with the laying of the tile.

Note that the entire process of setting tiles in mortar will go more smoothly if everything is kept damp during the process. Before beginning, spray the concrete slab well, soak the tiles in water and periodically lightly spray the section you are working on.

Mix the mortar according to the directions on the sack. Using a rectangular trowel, apply the mortar over the concrete slab, no more than 20 square feet at a time. For ceramic tiles, make the mortar bed 1/4 inch thick; for paver or quarry tiles, make the mortar bed 1/2 inch thick. Using a 2 by 4 longer than the width of the mortar bed, level it. (You'll need another pair of hands at the other side of the 2 by 4 to accomplish this.) Starting at one corner, gently press the tiles into damp mortar, leaving approximately 1/4 inch in between them. After you have laid several courses, lay a long straight board over the top of the tiles, checking to see if they are all level.

The precise geometry of this ceramic tile patio intentionally echoes the grid pattern of the surrounding fence.

Gently rap on the board to push any uneven tiles into place. Continue the process as outlined above until the patio is complete. Allow the mortar to set for 24 hours. Mix the mortar or grout mix according to the package directions, and spread into the joints using a rubber trowel. When the mortar or grout is almost dry, wipe off the excess with a large damp sponge and a fine mist of water. When complete, spray again with a fine mist of water, cover the patio with plastic sheeting, and allow to cure for a week.

You'll get maximum effect by matching the landscape building materials to the type of house you own. Here a Spanish tile terrace complements the Mediterranean-style house perfectly.

The ceramic tile of this enclosed patio underscores the seamless transition from indoors to outdoors.

DECK STYLES

Look carefully at the exterior of your house, taking note of any architectural details on railings, balusters, windows and roof lines. Can those details be re-created in the deck railings, stairs or handrails? Can the "apron" that surrounds the deck be finished in a way similar or complementary to the foundation of your house? If it's impossible to match the base of the deck with the foundation of the house, "ground" the deck by enclosing the bottom sides in some fashion. Lattice panels are great for this purpose and will complement almost any architectural style.

In addition to keeping the architectural style of your house in mind, there's one more important thing you can do to blend a new deck with a period-style house—namely, paint it—the mere suggestion of which brings howls of protest from

Because they are relatively non-slippery and water drains rapidly through them, wooden decks are one of the best surfaces for use next to swimming pools.

Wooden decks are ideal for use as "aprons" around spas, completely camouflaging their undersides.

those who admire lumber's natural weathered look and from those who fear that painting anything outdoors means constant upkeep. But a new generation of stains, specially formulated for outdoor use and available in a wide range of colors, will actually help preserve the wood. Ask at your local hardware or paint store for recommendations.

By staining the floor of the deck to match the color of the exterior walls of your house, and the railings to match the color of the trim, you will go a long way toward achieving a harmonious picture.

If you are contracting out the design and construction work, and your house has a distinct period style, be sure to discuss your desires with your contractor. Don't

assume that the contractor will automatically try to tie the deck to the house stylistically. And don't be tempted to buy a "package" deck, the design details of which may have nothing to do with the style of your house.

Pay close attention to a few details and you can design and build a deck that will be integral to your house, instead of looking like a tacked-on afterthought.

A deck is one of the best ways to significantly add to the living space in your garden.

Homeowners find they use patios and decks more frequently if they are located right next to the back door.

The design and construction of any deck can easily accommodate even large trees growing through their surface.

In addition to creating space for outdoor living, decks provide an effortless transition between indoors and out.

ANATOMY OF A DECK

Railing
Bench
Decking, usually 2 by 4 or 2 by 6 lumber
Steps
Apron
Stringers, usually 2 by 4 lumber
Joists, usually 2 by 6 lumber
Concrete piers, set in concrete

DECKS—THE RIGHT SIZE, THE RIGHT PLAN

As with any construction project, when building a patio, terrace or deck, the budget is a primary consideration. That said, when you are making plans for a patio or deck, bear in mind that one of the most common, after-the-fact complaints heard from homeowners is, "I wish we had made it bigger." The minimum space required by a table and a couple of chairs—with room to move around them—is approximately 120 square feet, or a 10-foot by 12-foot rectangle.

If you're like most people, you always feel a push-pull between your dreams and the realities of your budget. Whenever possible, err on the side of overbuilding, rather than underbuilding. In the long run, you'll probably be happier with the results.

To determine how much space a specific table and set of chairs will need, place them on a level surface. Sit down in one of the chairs and then push away from the table as you would normally do at the end of a meal. Mark the position of the rear legs of the chair, using a stake or a good-sized rock. Repeat this process on each side of the table, marking the position of the rear chair legs each time. Measure the distance between the markers, and then add 6 to 8 feet to the dimensions to leave enough space to walk behind the chairs when they are in a pulled-out position.

Bear in mind, most communities have building codes stipulating how close a patio or deck may be placed to your property line. Before finalizing your plans, acquaint yourself with any legal restrictions that may apply to your project. If you find that there's simply not enough room to satisfy both the legal requirements and your table and chairs, you may have to settle for a smaller outdoor dining set.

Outdoor areas for sitting and/or lounging have similar requirements. Again, the best place to start is with the actual measurements of the furniture you have in mind (note that even in mail-order catalogs this information is provided in the product description). Unlike a dining table and chairs, however, outdoor "sofas," chairs and chaises are more or less stationary and do not require space in addition to their "footprint," other than what's needed to comfortably maneuver through the area.

While it's true that your outdoor living area will be occupied by your entire family only a portion of the time, it's an excellent idea to plan for that situation from the beginning. Whenever possible, purchase a dining table large enough to accommodate everyone in your family—and then some, if friends or relatives are a frequent complement to your gatherings. And while most people are willing to relax their expectations somewhat in an outdoor setting, it's a hospitable gesture to include enough furniture in your outdoor living room to provide comfortable seating for everyone, just as you would in an indoor living room.

Owners tend to fall in love with their decks, their only questions being: "Why didn't we build it sooner?" and "Why didn't we build it a little bigger?"

GRADE-LEVEL DECKS

Grade-level decks are the easiest of all decks to construct, well within the range of do-it-yourselfers with moderate carpentry skills. Because they float just a few inches above the surrounding soil level, there's no need for the rather complicated task of building steps. And because they are so close to the ground, you can probably dispense with the need for any protective railing. You can build a grade-level deck right next to your house, or position it anywhere in your yard that a flat, level surface is desired.

Lumber yards and home improvement centers carry a wide range of helpful hardware for deck building. Look for a variety of brackets that make hanging joists onto beams an easy task, as well as special brackets which connect beams to posts.

The Basic Elements of a Grade-Level Deck

1 Using stakes and string, lay out the deck, measuring carefully. Use stakes to mark the locations of the posts or piers.

2 If the top of the deck is to be just above the level of the soil, excavate the soil to accommodate the height of the posts or piers.

3 In cold winter regions, dig postholes below the frost line, fill with 3 inches of gravel, and then fill with concrete, making sure posts are level.

4 Let concrete cure for at least 24 hours. Mark all four sides of the posts at the correct height and make a level cut.

5 Position two 2 x 8's on top of the posts to form sturdy perimeter beams. Make sure they are level and then attach to the posts with straps or brackets.

6 Using special joist hanging brackets (attached to beams), position the joists so they are level with the top of the beams.

7 Nail the deck boards to the joists, using two nails at each intersection. Keep spacing even between boards with a small plywood spacer or nail.

8 When all of the decking is nailed into place, use a chalk line to mark the straight sides of the deck. Nail a guide in place for the straightest possible edge, then trim the decking to be flush.

9 If desired, dress up the cut edge of the deck with a decorative molding. Use mitered joints to keep spliced molding secure.

RAISED DECKS

Although the basic deck-building principles are the same, raised decks present a slightly more difficult project than your average grade-level deck. Be aware that almost all communities have building codes and guidelines governing these types of decks. To save many a future headache, be sure to check with your community's building departments before embarking on any raised-deck building project.

One of the best things about a raised deck is the way it creates a stable, level outdoor living surface "in thin air," regardless of how uneven the terrain beneath it might be. But because of its height, greater strength is demanded in the construction of a raised deck, usually requiring bolts and lag screws in place of the nails used with grade-level decks. In addition, once you get more than a few inches off the ground, some kind of railing will be required (by law), as will stairs leading to and from the deck. Once these factors are taken into consideration, many homeowners opt to have a raised deck professionally constructed.

As a final touch, most owners of raised decks choose to camouflage the sides so the underside of the construction cannot be seen. The popular material for this is 4-by 8-foot panels of lattice, a solution which works quite well. Be aware, however, there are many grades of lattice; for longevity and ease of maintenance, always favor lattice panels constructed of the sturdiest lumber.

The Basic Elements of a Raised Deck

1 Using stakes and string, lay out the deck (as shown on page 50). Use stakes to mark the locations of the posts or piers.

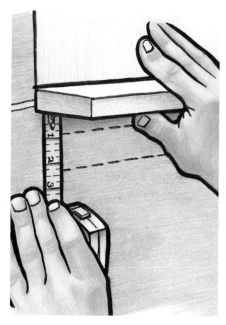

2 Make a mark on the side of the house indicating the top of the deck surface. Note: You can construct the deck so there is a step down from the interior of the house, or level with interior floor.

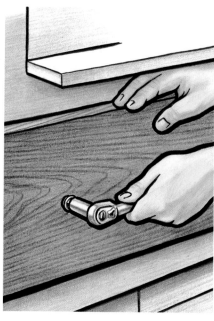

3 Attach the ledger board to the side of the house using lag screws and washers, first making sure the ledger, itself, is level even though the house may not be. Make sure the ledger is extremely secure.

4 In cold winter regions, dig postholes below the frost line, fill with 6 inches of gravel, and then fill with concrete, making sure posts are level. Let concrete cure for at least 24 hours.

5 Using a board and level, mark the desired height of the posts by putting one end of the board on top of the ledger and the other against the post. Make sure the board is level before marking the post.

6 Mark all four sides of the posts at the correct height and make a level cut with a chain saw or circular saw.

7 Position two 2 x 8's on either side of the posts to form sturdy perimeter beams. Make sure they are level and then attach to the posts with bolts all the way through the posts and beams.

8 Attach joist hanging brackets to the ledger board and toenail the joists to the top of beams. For sturdier construction, notch the tops of the posts to accept the joists and use screws to secure them in place.

9 Nail the deck boards to the joists, starting next to the house, using two nails at each intersection. Keep spacing even between boards with a small plywood spacer or nail. Trim the edges of the deck as shown in Step 8 on page 51.

From simple to complex, overheads provide comfort and beauty for outdoor living.

OVERHEAD PROTECTION

The most beautiful overhead protection in any backyard setting is the dense, leafy canopy provided by a mature shade tree. Unfortunately, the place where you'd really like to sit in the shade may not be graced by such a tree or, conversely, the place where the tree is growing may not be where you want the protection. These are situations when, if you want immediate overhead protection, it must be constructed rather than grown.

Outdoor overhead protection is used as a shield against the sun or rain, or to keep from being directly in your neighbor's line of sight, especially from second-story windows. If you don't mind the rain, there are many construction options, with lattice and lath being perennial favorites. Depending on how much sun you want to allow through, the lath work can be constructed in a tight or loose design. Either way, the resulting shade pattern below will create a dappled effect, pleasant for both plants and people.

Or consider having an awning made. In addition to standard canvas or vinyl materials (which offer protection from the rain), many great awning products are avail-able, including some that allow sunlight and air to filter through.

If you need total protection from the elements, what you build overhead will be more like the roof on your house. In fact, simply copying whatever your roof is made from, whether it's cedar shakes or composition shingles, is one of the best ways to visually tie this outdoor structure to the house.

Both options—latticework and awnings—are classics. They have been used for generations in a wide variety of settings, to the point where either looks right at home with almost any architectural style.

OVERHEAD OPTIONS

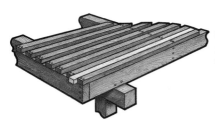

Evenly-spaced pieces of lath make for an interesting shadow pattern below, one with just enough sun and shade.

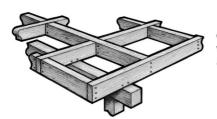

The more open "egg crate" design is best used in regions where hot sun and strong winds are not frequent problems.

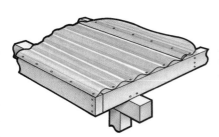

Translucent corrugated fiberglass panels allow filtered light to pass through, but no rain nor ventilation. This is probably not your best overhead option.

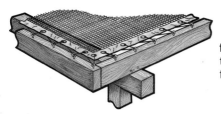

Canvas is an old-time favorite for overhead protection. Steer toward the newer acrylic fabrics for longest life.

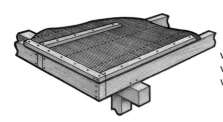

Shade cloth comes in a variety of weaves, supplying varying degrees of shade and water and wind protection.

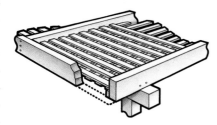

A double layer of lath, laid perpendicular to each other, provides fairly dense shade, with ample ventilation.

MADE IN THE SHADE

High on the list of priorities for comfortable outdoor living is at least one shade tree. Lucky is the person who inherits a house with a beautiful, strategically located, mature shade tree. If you're not that lucky, your consolation lies in being able to choose the type of tree you want, and in planting it exactly where you want it.

Faced with a treeless yard, the feature most people ask for when shopping for trees is anything fast growing. While this request is perfectly understandable, beware. In virtually every part of the country, the fastest-growing shade trees adapted to that area also have more than their fair share of drawbacks. For some, it is susceptibility to a regional disease. Others have weak limb structures that break easily in storms, and some trees are short-lived and go into decline shortly after they reach the size where they provide that much-sought-after shade.

Before planting any shade tree, consult with the staff of your local nursery, garden center or agricultural extension service. Ask for a list of recommended trees and find out as much as you can about their traits, both good and bad. In the long run, you may be better off with a slightly slower-growing tree, but one that will mature into a healthy, long-lived specimen.

Some of the best and most widely adapted trees for providing shade include: the Norway maple, scarlet maple, European beech, ginkgo, liquidambar, pin oak and American linden.

Norway maple.

Gingko.

LATTICE & OTHER OPEN OVERHEADS

The basic definition of an open overhead is one that lets the elements—sun, wind and rain—through in varying degrees.

An open overhead does not so much protect you from the elements as it does modify them. Once the basic construction for a shade structure (which is nothing more than an upright post and horizontal beams) is complete, a wide variety of materials can be put into place to provide various degrees of protection.

With just the right mixture of sun and shade, this outdoor dining room is the perfect place for an al fresco meal.

These include lattice, lath, bamboo, shade cloth and canvas.

In the old days, constructing lattice was a tedious job; today, pre-made lattice panels are readily available, most often in 4-foot by 8-foot dimensions. Be aware that these panels vary widely in quality from very flimsy to what is called "architectural grade." If longevity is important, always favor the best quality materials. Any lattice panel can be quickly stapled or nailed onto the shade structure's rafters, creating almost instant shade.

Lath is the material that lattice is constructed from and is available in lengths up to 12 feet. Individual lath strips are nailed onto the rafters, in parallel fashion, with the width separating them determining the amount of sun and shade below. If you want the same effect, but using heavier lumber, 1- by 2-inch boards work well and last much longer than lath.

Bamboo is available in rolls generally 6 feet in height and 12 or more feet in length. Although usually used as an inexpensive, temporary fencing, this material also works as a fast means of achieving shade when merely stapled to overhead rafters. But it may not last more than one or two seasons.

Shade cloth is a woven plastic material, usually 6 feet wide, and sold in rolls. The amount of shade it provides is determined by the density of its weave; most garden centers will offer it in three or more densities. It can simply be stapled onto overhead rafters, and should last two seasons or more.

Canvas has long been a favorite for providing shade in outdoor settings. For generations, the only choice was heavy cotton. New acrylic material has the look and feel of canvas but is not subject to rot or mildew. Available in a wide variety of colors, patterns and widths, canvas is a very versatile material. Most often fashioned into awnings by professionals, it can also simply be tacked into place.

Depending on the angle of the sun, even a narrow band of lattice can provide shade right where you need it.

Lumber, laid on its edge, creates a shadow pattern which changes dramatically throughout the day, depending on the angle of the sun.

A simple lath house, constructed of pre-made 4- by 8-foot lattice panels, makes a wonderful environment for growing plants.

The corner of this deck, high in the treetops, is sheltered from the weather with a pergola-like structure.

When you want plenty of light but complete protection from the elements, consider adding plexiglass panels to your overhead.

This solid overhead provides protection from frequent summer rains, while the ceiling fan creates a gentle breeze.

SOLID OVERHEADS

A solid overhead provides complete protection from sun and rain, important considerations in climates where either or both make outdoor living uncomfortable. Be aware, however, that a solid overhead will trap heat and humidity, so you will probably want to keep the sides of the shade structure more or less open to encourage a free flow of air.

The most visually harmonious solid overhead shade structures are those that employ the same design details and construction materials as the house, whether attached to the house or not. Although this is an expensive project, many homeowners consider it a worthwhile investment, both in terms of beauty and comfort.

Vinylized canvas is another option for a solid overhead that, when constructed by an awning specialist, can be very attractive. The material does not allow rain or sunlight through, tends to be long-lasting, and needs only a simple frame made of metal pipe to secure it in place. True, severe storms may take their effect on this material, but most homeowners view that potential as a reasonable trade-off for an awning's relatively inexpensive cost. And one of the best things about awnings is the ease with which they complement virtually any architectural style.

ANATOMY OF AN OVERHEAD

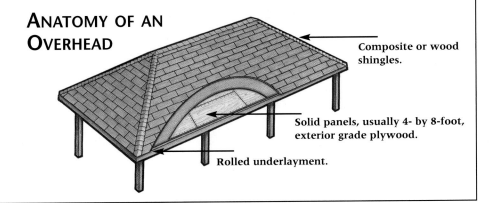

Composite or wood shingles.

Solid panels, usually 4- by 8-foot, exterior grade plywood.

Rolled underlayment.

ARBORS & PERGOLAS

Some overhead structures are intended not so much as protection from the elements, but as support for vining plants—definitely a case of the best of both worlds: immediate protection provided by a built structure combined with the eventual leafy overhead that would take a shade tree decades to produce.

Two of the most popular structures for vining plants are arbors and pergolas. Although the two are sometimes confused, a pergola is a freestanding, semi-open-roofed structure ("semi-open" means there are a few connecting pieces of lumber for the vines to attach themselves to), while an arbor is most often constructed over a patio or terrace, or a walk-way connecting one building or living area with another.

The key to success with either an arbor or a pergola is to build it to last—through both the rigors of weather and the long-term effects of serving as a support for rapacious vining plants. Choose the heaviest lumber consistent with the scale of your yard, and use long screws (instead of nails) to hold the timbers together. If you plan on painting or staining the structure, do it right the first time: it's practically impossible to re-paint an arbor or pergola once it's covered with a vine, and most vining plants, such as wis-teria, grapevines, honeysuckle, trumpet vine and the like, are rampant growers.

Although most arbors and pergolas are constructed of fairly heavy lumber, more temporary structures can be built of flexible branches cut from trees, the most popular being willow. Although not permanent, any flexible branch can be formed into a variety of fanciful and romantic designs, including Gothic arches and Oriental-inspired patterns. All that is necessary is to stick the long branches upright into the ground, and then secure lateral branches with heavy twine.

Although not nearly as romantic, arbors and pergolas may be constructed of metal pipe, using threaded couplers to make connections. If painted a dark hue and planted with vining plants, these structures can be as attractive as they are practical.

To avoid damage, any arbor planted with vines will need to be constructed of heavy timbers.

A flat-roofed pergola adds architectural interest to this low-maintenance landscape.

Few things are as charming as a vine-covered arbor arching over a garden gate.

Arbors run the gamut, from the refined elegance of a white-painted arch to the rustic simplicity of rough-sawn timbers.

GAZEBOS

The gazebo is closely associated in this country with the Victorian era, and many of today's gazebos retain their gingerbread character. Considering, however, that gazebos are by their very nature fanciful, there's no reason to stick with a particular architectural style or even tie the architecture of the gazebo to that of your house.

Gazebos and fantasy are natural partners. If you've always wanted a gazebo that looked like a Japanese tea house, even though you live in a two-story Tudor, there's nothing to stop you from making that fantasy a reality.

An often overlooked function of a gazebo is to serve as a protected spot for outdoor dining. Because most gazebos are constructed with seating around the interior perimeter, all that's needed is a table. Any meal becomes a memorable event when taken in a gazebo, and it's perfect for special occasions such as birthday parties (gazebos look great done up in balloons and streamers) or a late-night, just-the-two-of-you dinner, with lots of votive candles, small portions of extravagant food, some flowers from the garden ... well ... you get the picture.

Given the amount of architectural detail most gazebos contain—not to mention their frequently unusual shape—they can be a construction nightmare and represent a considerable financial investment. To be most effective, most gazebos are constructed over wooden decking instead of a concrete pad. For their relatively small size, gazebos

Outfitted with comfortable furnishings, there are few places more pleasant than a gazebo.

take an extraordinary attention to detail to look their best. For this reason most homeowners who desire a gazebo in their backyard are best off purchasing a complete kit, or having the entire project professionally built.

An adult version of a treehouse, this gazebo playfully provides an overlook of the entire backyard.

Acting like a lure to visiting guests, this artfully perched gazebo takes full advantage of the surrounding views.

A large pond is perfectly complemented by a simple gazebo, the perfect spot to reflect on the surrounding natural beauty.

OUTBUILDINGS & OTHER BACKYARD HIDEAWAYS

At the turn of the 20th century practically all backyards had a least one outbuilding, usually at the far end of the lot. Today these structures have been largely replaced by prefabricated metal sheds, notably lacking in charm and certainly the last place anyone might think of for using as a hideaway—one of their better uses. Sure, you can use an outbuilding as a place to store garden equipment, out-of-season outdoor furniture and the like, but these little structures can also serve as homey places to put a potting shed, tend to a hobby or just as a quiet place to get away from it all.

Building an outbuilding is a straightforward proposition, demanding only the most rudimentary of carpentry skills, well within the range of the average do-it-yourselfer. If your skill level happens to fall below average, a carpenter will be able to build the structure in just a few days' time if supplied with some simple drawings and dimensions.

Before starting on such a project, check with your local building department to ensure that your project meets with its requirements, paying particular attention to setback requirements (the number of feet between a building and your property lines). That said, the most suitable place for an outbuilding is usually at the far end of the yard where it won't assume undue prominence.

A 10- by 12-foot building is more than adequate for most purposes. Start by pouring a concrete slab (see page 40), making sure to include the anchor bolts. Walls are formed using standard framing techniques and attached to the concrete slab using the anchor bolts. If you're lucky, you may be able to find pre-made roofing joists at the lumberyard, or construct your own. External paneling is available in a wide variety of styles, sold in 4- by

With the addition of translucent plastic panels in the roof, the owner of this outbuilding gained a greenhouse along with a place to store tools.

Garden sheds can take many forms. For all their practical utility, their design can be as interesting and fanciful as you care to make them.

8-foot sheets that go up in a hurry. Apply rolled roofing over an external-grade plywood roof and, with the exception of windows and a door, you've got yourself a weatherproof shed.

Once your new outbuilding is constructed, take a few steps to incorporate it into its garden setting. Trimmed lattice panels can be nailed to the exterior walls as support for vining plants. A small arbor over the door, covered with a climbing rose or other flowering vine, has a timeless appeal. Plant a few trees around the shed to frame it and visually anchor it to the landscape. Add a comfortable wooden bench next to the shed—and you may find that it becomes your favorite spot for lingering over lunch or your morning coffee.

With its classical design, this simple storage shed looks a little like an ancient Greek or Roman temple.

Very much a focal point in its own right, this attractive outbuilding also serves the practical function of providing weatherproof storage for all types of garden tools and equipment.

A room of one's own: Few spaces are as satisfying as one where you can pursue a hobby to your heart's content.

HOBBY STUDIOS

Consider making a playhouse big enough to function as a hobby studio for eventual use by adults.

Old-fashioned outbuildings were originally intended for practical uses, from tool storage to use as a potting shed. But over time, many of these simple sheds developed into something decidedly more personal and unique. With each passing year, it wasn't unusual for the little building to take on more of the owner's personality and for the owner to spend more time in his or her miniature home-away-from-home. Postcards and calendar pictures might be thumbtacked to the unpainted walls. Perhaps a collection of smooth granite stones was placed on view in the windowsill. An odd assortment of artifacts, unearthed while digging in the garden, might be set upon one corner of the workbench.

In many ways, this type of outbuilding can become a grown-up version of that fort you may have had as a child—a place of refuge that is part of, yet apart from, that place called home. In an era when everyone seems to be perennially short on space, an extra spot out there in the back of the yard might be just the thing to provide a little breathing room, the place you go to when you need to be alone.

When you use an outbuilding for a hobby such as oil painting, pottery making or model building, you enjoy the added benefit of being able to leave your work in progress, along with all of its attendant tools and supplies, rather than having to gather everything up off the kitchen table in time for tomorrow morning's breakfast. Activities notorious for disturbing others—such as drum practice, voice lessons or cigar smoking—can be carried out in an outbuilding in harmless obscurity and delight.

The key is to keep the project modest. Your tool shed sanctuary can be constructed from second-hand lumber, windows and doors from the salvage yard, and the barest of amenities. Electricity is probably a must, but running water, indoor plumbing, heat or air-conditioning, carpeting, rain gutters and downspouts, insulation and paint for the walls all fall into the "optional" category. Don't fix up the place too much; the appeal of these small buildings is often in their rustic character. Once you start using your backyard studio, you'll quickly discover what's essential and what's not. If you find yourself spending weekends and evenings there, you may want to add a simple electric radiator for heat. A few panels of sheetrock will dress up and lighten the interior in a hurry, and you may want to add some type of flooring over the concrete to warm the place up a bit. Take your time and add improvements in stages and you'll end up with a truly comfortable, customized studio.

Kids don't stay little forever, so if you are going to go to the effort of building a playhouse for your children, do it now.

CHAPTER 3
CREATING PRIVACY

It's a simple but often overlooked fact that home gardens are, and were always meant to be, private places. This applies whether the privacy is achieved by owning all the land to the horizon or, for most homeowners, by enclosing their small plot in some way. Somewhat surprisingly, there are a number of neighborhoods (indeed, whole geographic regions) where fences between houses are forbidden, either by covenant or custom. And even if you live in an area where fences, walls or hedges are permitted, you may still be concerned that a fence or wall will somehow offend the neighbors on the other side. But unless you feel protected, you won't feel comfortable. And if you don't feel comfortable in your yard, you'll probably spend very little time out there.

FENCES

A fence should be viewed as a permanent addition to the landscape and, as such, should be built as sturdily as possible, using the highest quality building materials possible. Few things distract from a property's look more than a shabby, run-down fence. Instead of merely ordering the fencing material sight unseen and having it delivered, it pays to go to the lumberyard and handpick the materials yourself.

If you plan to grow vines on your fence—which is a fast and effective way of incorporating it into the rest of the landscape— pay extra attention to the sturdiness of the structure. Almost all vines will, over time, work their way in between boards and posts, usually with destructive results. If vining plants are a part of your fencing plans, use screws, rather than nails, to hold all parts of the fence together—including the fence boards to the rails.

If the fence is built on unlevel terrain, you'll be more pleased with the results if you either stair-step the fence down (or up) to compensate for the grade (keeping the tops of the individual sections of fence parallel and level), or keep the top of the fence all one level, compensating for the grade at the bottom of the fence. A fence built at the same angle as the incline of the terrain has a visually disturbing effect and should be avoided.

Graceful curves and a lattice overlay turn this solid fence into a design statement.

Short fences may not provide privacy, but they can visually define one part of the garden from another.

The plainest of fences or walls can be incorporated into the landscape by means of paint and a variety of vining plants.

By arranging bricks to leave a regular pattern of open spaces, an interesting peek-a-boo effect is achieved.

FENCE INSIGHTS

Fences, as opposed to walls or hedges, are the fastest and least expensive way to ensure privacy in a yard. If, however, you have the funds and desire to build a stone, masonry, or brick wall, by all means do so. They are picturesque and appropriate to houses of almost any architectural style. Or, if you don't mind waiting the several years it takes a hedge to grow tall and thick enough to provide privacy, go right ahead and plant one. Hedges, too, are complementary to virtually any architectural style, and there's nothing quite as pretty in an outdoor setting as a living wall of even, clipped green.

To ensure the results you want from any barrier, take a couple of 8-foot-tall stakes, a long length of clothesline or strong twine, a handful of clothespins, and a couple of old sheets or lightweight blankets. Pound the stakes into the ground at either end of the line separating the yards, and tie the clothesline to the stakes at the height you think you want. Next, clip the sheets (or what have you) to the line with the clothespins, and then step back to the part of the garden where you want the greatest privacy. If you can't see your neighbors, you know how tall to make your fence.

If both you and your neighbors agree that a fence would be mutually beneficial, it is customary for both parties to share the cost of the fence. If so, the fence should be built directly on the property line. If you want a fence and your neighbor doesn't, you'll have to forge ahead on your own as diplomatically as possible, paying for it yourself and locating it clearly on your side of the property line.

WOODEN FENCES

Picket fences can be constructed in a number of styles and heights, all of which display a familiar charm and appeal.

At one time, the only commonly available wooden fence style was the familiar "dog-eared" design. Fencing contractors and do-it-yourself outlets now offer any number of pleasing options.

As you make your decision about what type of fence to build, remember that a fence is a significant and long-lasting feature of any landscape. It pays to go the extra mile and build a fence that is both visually and architecturally appealing (from both your side of the fence and your neighbors')—not to mention one that will last a generation or two.

As you explore your options with wooden fencing, keep in mind this important point: a wooden fence need not be solid to perform its job (and there will be some instances where a solid board fence will make an outdoor space feel too confined). Any of the "openwork" designs shown on the opposite page will keep dogs out, kids in and effectively screen the neighbor's view of your private space. And any vertical barrier—even if it is not a solid one—placed in the foreground of a landscape causes the eye to stop on it, rather than the scene beyond. For example, an open lattice fence placed to block an offending view of the neighbor's garage may still allow some of the offending view to peek through. Luckily, however, human perception is such that we focus on the lattice fence and not the object behind it.

With so many options to choose from—from lattice panels to an overlying grid—it's no longer necessary to settle for a plain board fence.

FENCE OPTIONS

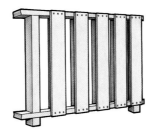

Board fences can be constructed with all the boards on one side, or alternating from one side to the other, which increases air circulation.

Where privacy is the goal, a solid panel fence may be the answer. The addition of overlying lattice can dress up its plain exterior.

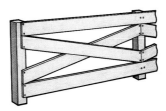

The classic post-and-board fence is a good choice for properties where privacy is not a concern.

Picket fences, usually not more than 4 or 5 feet tall, are great for keeping dogs out and toddlers in.

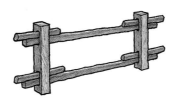

The post-and-rail design is one of the simplest of all fences, excellent for defining one part of the garden from another with a minimum of material.

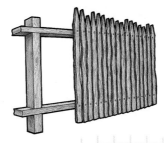

The so-called "grapestake" fence offers a rustic, informal appeal while providing complete privacy.

A picket fence may not add much privacy, but it clearly delineates the difference between public and private spaces.

Before you begin a fencing project, check out local building codes and community covenants to see what is allowed and what isn't. In some cases, communities have considerable say with regard to fence height, building materials and colors.

Fence building falls well within the abilities of most do-it-yourselfers, requiring only basic tools and equipment. If the fence is a long one, however, you may want to rent a power posthole digger to make that tedious job go as quickly as possible. Begin the project with stakes and strings, marking the position of the fence. Upright posts (usually 4 x 4 rot-resistant lumber) are spaced every 6 to 8 feet along the fence line, at even intervals. Set posts in concrete; use temporary braces to hold the posts level on all sides as the concrete sets. Top and bottom rails (usually 2 x 4 lumber) can be toenailed into position or put into place using special galvanized rail clips available at lumberyards. Once the top and bottom rails are in position, it's a simple matter of nailing the fence boards in place.

For the greatest longevity, all lumber for posts and rails should be of construction-grade heart redwood or cedar (both of which are naturally rot-resistant) or ground-contact, pressure-treated wood. Use hot-dipped galvanized nails and fittings to keep rust to a minimum.

MASONRY FENCES

Brick, stone and stucco-covered walls are the most long-lasting of all garden additions. They are relatively expensive and time-consuming to build, but pay off handsomely in the long run in terms of good looks and increased property value. All three materials are considered "traditional" and combine wonderfully with traditional architectural styles such as Tudor, Mediterranean and rustic cottages. Because they are so architectural in appearance and permanent, great care should be taken in their design, making sure they present a harmonious scene—house and wall as one continuous style.

Brick and stone walls, because of the small size of the individual building units, can be considered a do-it-yourself project—if a fairly demanding one. But once you have the basic construction technique down, as shown on the opposite page, it's just a matter of repetition, patience and muscle. And don't forget, even with all of its heavy solidness, a brick wall needn't be constructed with a solid design; check out the "pierced" pattern (shown on page 71).

Masonry walls covered with stucco are definitely not a do-it-yourself project, but are nonetheless good alternatives to brick and stone. New construction techniques allow stucco to be applied (usually "shot" onto the vertical surface using a pressurized hose) to a lightweight structure. Once it has cured, it's amazingly strong and long-lasting. The stucco itself can be colored to match or complement the color of your house, creating a harmonious look, and its rough surface provides just enough grip for a variety of vining plants.

All masonry walls begin with a level concrete footing, the same width as that of the ultimate wall and as long, 6 to 8 inches thick. Where freezing and thawing temperatures occur, the concrete footing is placed over a 4-inch layer of gravel, used to promote good drainage. Once this "pad" has cured, you can begin building off it, using either brick or stone, with the assurance that your wall will remain level and sound for many years to come.

Once completed, the look of any masonry wall can be improved by the addition of greenery, usually in the form of vines. Some people opt for a delicate tracery of branches here and there, while others prefer vines with dense coverage. Wisteria, trumpet vine, ivy and clematis are just a few favorites that attach themselves readily to any masonry surface, softening its appearance with leafy green and, in some cases, colorful flowers.

Somewhat surprisingly, any brick or masonry fence can be constructed to artfully accommodate curves.

This stucco-covered wall acts primarily as a retaining wall, but makes a pleasant design statement at the same time.

Brick walls can be built in a dizzying array of styles, from the very plain to the very complex.

The most beautiful—and most expensive—of walls are those constructed of stone.

STONE BONDING PATTERNS

Untrimmed stone, laid in a random pattern, without mortar.

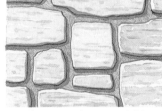

Rough-squared stones, laid without coursing.

Square-cut stone with regular coursing.

Untrimmed stone, laid in a random pattern, with the addition of mortar.

Rough-squared stones, with horizontal coursing.

Square-cut stone with random coursing.

Depending on the type of plant used, hedges can assume a wide variety of heights—from short to tall—and can be clipped into almost any shape.

HEDGES—FORMAL & INFORMAL

No question about it: a mature, well-clipped green hedge is one of the most beautiful "walls" possible in any landscape. And depending on what size they are when they are purchased, hedges can be quite economical. They do, however, require several years, along with regular pruning and shearing, to achieve their goal.

Once mature, hedges make an attractive backdrop for flower borders and the like, but if you're looking for physical (not just visual) enclosure, be aware that pets and children are remarkably adept at finding their way both in and out of hedges.

If you'd prefer something less formal than a clipped hedge, groupings of small evergreen trees and large shrubs can screen a view and create privacy. If the plants are chosen for their contrasting shapes, foliage texture and color, and heights, such a grouping makes for an interesting addition to the landscape—

The look of a hedge can be created by allowing a vine to grow over a low-growing fence.

with a lot less work than a traditional hedge.

Most hedges require annual or semi-annual pruning, usually in spring or summer, after new growth has stopped. To keep lower branches from becoming bare of foliage, trim formal hedges so they

are narrower at the top; this shape allows sunlight to reach the entire surface of the hedge. Feed hedge plantings once each spring with a complete fertilizer.

The following plants are excellent candidates for hedge plantings:

GREAT HEDGE PLANTS

Rose hedge.

Abelia x grandiflora. Glossy abelia. Evergreen in mild climates; deciduous in the North. Graceful arching branches do not need pruning. Pale pink flowers all summer. Hardy to Zone 6. Grows to 6 feet tall. Space plants 4 feet apart.

Berberis x mentorensis. Barberry. Semi-evergreen with dark green smallish leaves and very dense habit of growth. Hardy to Zone 5. Grows to 6 feet tall. Space plants 30 inches apart.

Berberis thunbergii. Japanese barberry. Very hardy deciduous shrub. Good fall color and winter berries. Hardy to Zone 4. Grows to 5 feet tall. Space plants 3 feet apart.

Buxus species. Boxwood. Classic plants for hedges. Small-leaved, evergreen, densely branched shrubs. Many varieties, all well suited for hedges. Hardiness and spacing depend on species. Depending on variety, boxwoods grow from 1 to 6 feet tall.

Ilex crenata. Japanese holly. Small-leaved, evergreen, densely branched shrubs. Slow growing. Hardy to Zone 6. Space plants 3 feet apart.

Laurus nobilis. Grecian laurel. Evergreen shrub or small tree of great distinction. Slow growing. Hardy to Zone 7-8. Will grow to 30 feet tall but can be held at virtually any height with pruning. Space plants 4 feet apart.

Ligustrum species. Privet. One of the classic hedge plants. Many varieties, all well suited for hedges. Small-leaved, evergreen, densely branched shrubs. Can be pruned into almost any shape. Hardiness and spacing depend on species, but most are hardy to at least Zone 7. Height depends on variety, with some growing 12 feet tall or more. Can be held at almost any height with regular pruning.

Rosa rugosa. Ramanas rose. Very tough, hardy deciduous shrub with prickly stems. Excellent for use in difficult locations. Single or double flowers throughout spring and summer in shades of white, yellow, pink and dark red. Large red fruits follow after flowers fade. Hardy to Zone 2. Will grow to 5 feet tall. Space plants 2 feet apart.

Taxus species. Yew. Classic evergreen hedge plant with fine, needle-like foliage. Reliable even in shaded conditions. Slow growing. Height and spacing depend on species, but all can be held to almost any height with regular pruning. Hardiness depends on species, but some are hardy all the way to Zone 2.

HEDGE TIPS

Shaping a Hedge
Shaping a hedge is a multi-year project, with the first three years being the most important.

Year One: Let the hedge fill out to a natural form, then trim it about a quarter to a third of the way back, slightly tapered towards the top.

Year Two: Once again, let the hedge grow out a ways, then cut it back about a quarter of the way, gradually allowing it to assume its mature size.

Year Three: At this point, your hedge should be dense and full, ready to be maintained at its ultimate size with regular, minor trimmings.

Let the Sun Shine In

Here is a correctly trimmed or sheared hedge with the bottom wider than the top, allowing sunlight on the entire hedge.

If the top of the hedge is wider than the bottom, it will keep the sun from reaching the bottom, ultimately causing dieback.

Informal or Formal?

An informally pruned hedge does not rely on precise shearing for its appeal.

Formal hedges require several prunings each year to maintain their geometric appearance.

Boxwood hedge.

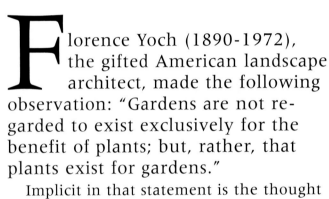

CHAPTER 4

GREEN GOODS

Florence Yoch (1890-1972), the gifted American landscape architect, made the following observation: "Gardens are not regarded to exist exclusively for the benefit of plants; but, rather, that plants exist for gardens."

Implicit in that statement is the thought that gardens exist for people first, and for plants second. True, a backyard without plants would be a dismal sight, but one without people would have no reason to exist. Not everyone is interested in becoming an avid gardener, and not even all those who are interested have the time. Still, you can have a beautiful backyard without becoming a slave to gardening, especially if you are careful in your selection of plants.

HOW TO CHOOSE PLANTS

When it comes time to select plants for their landscape, most people start with a list of favorite plants. If you're looking for the least amount of upkeep, this is not the way to go about planting your garden.

Every geographic and climatic region of the country has plants well suited to its particular conditions. These are grasses, annuals, perennials, shrubs, vines and trees that display an admirable willingness to grow. They may not be the most unusual plants; in fact, most of them will be quite common. But a common plant that is in thriving condition is far more attractive and easy to maintain than a rare plant that only struggles along.

The more familiar you are with the plants that grow in your area, the better you will be able to create a good-looking landscape. Take note of plants that appeal to you in other gardens. If you don't know their names, ask the owner, or take a small leaf sample to your local nursery or garden center for identification.

Once you know the names of the plants, set about to learn as much as you can about them: their water, soil, fertilizer and climate requirements, their natural form, the mature height and width, whether they prefer sunny or shaded conditions, or any other characteristic that might be important in your particular situation. Above all, determine whether the plants that catch your eye are considered finicky or easy to grow.

The wisest course is to stick with plants that are the easiest to grow—the sure bets. In addition to choosing plants appropriate to your region, select individual plants well suited to the exact location in which you intend to plant them. When you go to the nursery or garden center, know the exposure of each of your planting sites: Does a particular site receive only morning sun, hot afternoon sun from 2 o'clock on or dappled sunlight under a large deciduous tree? Explain the growing conditions to the salesperson, describe how big the area is, what the soil is like and then—if you don't have your own list—ask to see appropriate plants for each specific area.

When choosing trees or shrubs, select only those plants that will fit physically, when mature, into the allotted space. For example, if you have roughly a 3-foot-diameter bare spot between two shrubs, don't choose a plant that ultimately grows 6 feet wide. Matching the plant to the space available will all but eliminate pruning, and your plants will be allowed to achieve their natural form rather than some abstract geometric shape resulting from repeated trimmings.

If the plant selection process sounds like it takes a fair amount of research and effort, it does. But you don't have to be the one to go to the effort or do the research. Most reputable nurseries will provide you with a custom planting plan, usually free of charge, if you agree to purchase the plants from their nursery. In most cases, this is a fair trade-off. Just be sure to let the salesperson know that you want plants with a marked willingness to grow in your location, and then leave the selection process in his or her capable hands.

Your first step in purchasing quality plants is locating a reputable nursery or garden center, the best of which only handle top-quality, healthy nursery stock, usually with a guarantee.

Aside from that initial step, look for plants with good, vibrant leaf color and evidence of new growth. If you carefully slide a plant out of its container, you should be able to see some white roots at the edges of the soil, not a tangled mass of roots running round the outside, indicating root-bound conditions. Select trees with a balanced crown and no crossing branches. If there's a choice between a plant that is in bud and one in full flower, always favor the one in the bud stage as it is likely to perform better in the long run.

The most effective plantings are often the simplest, relying on the mass planting of only a few different kinds of plants rather than a complex combination of "one of this, and one of that."

If your heart is set on a perennial border, but you have a limited time to devote to it, select only those plants known as "willing performers."

In place of upkeep, plants chosen carefully for their site will only demand admiration.

Every garden center is full of temptations, so it's a good idea to know exactly what you want to buy before you leave the house.

A classic example of hardy, willing-to-grow plants: sedum 'Autumn Joy,' rudbeckia and Russian sage.

THE LAWN CONTROVERSY

Much has been said and written about whether or not Americans should rethink their passion for the home lawn. There is general agreement that where summer rains are adequate and a well-adapted variety of grass is grown, lawns make perfect sense. Unfortunately, geographic areas where summer rains are adequate enough to support a lush, green stand of grass are few and far between in this country.

While we acknowledge the validity of those points, no surface is better suited to outdoor living and game playing than a grass lawn. Viewed from that perspective, the bigger the lawn, the better! The most practical and thoughtful opinions have suggested that a lawn is well worth the energy and expense it requires, in any region of the country, if it is actively used as

Big fun on the lawn.

a surface for outdoor living and playing. If, however, you do not intend to use the lawn for game playing and entertaining, by all means consider planting another type of groundcover, one well adapted to your area. Once groundcovers are established, they require far less maintenance than lawns do. Groundcovers make perfect sense when all you require is an even visual expanse of green to fill in the area between the house and the fence. Some of the best ground covers for lawn substitutes (which can take some foot traffic) include blue sedge (*Carex flacca*), chamomile (*Chamaemelum nobile*), dicondra (*Dicondra micrantha*), Hippocrepis comosa, lippia (*Phyla nodiflora*), Irish or Scotch moss (*Sagina subulata*), and Korean grass (*Zoysia tenuifolia*).

Lawns are extremely versatile groundcovers, with the ability to cover flat, sloped or terraced yards with equal agility.

It is possible to have a good-looking lawn without becoming a slave to its maintenance—just see the sidebar at right.

COMMONSENSE LAWN CARE

If you determine that a grass lawn makes sense for your yard, but you live in a climate ill-suited to supporting it naturally, there are four steps you can take to reduce its high-maintenance requirements and all but eliminate any negative environmental impact.

Step 1: Instead of bagging the lawn clippings, let them compost in place, right on the lawn. Recent research has shown that leaving the clippings on the lawn actually benefits the soil and the lawn. As the clippings decompose, they improve the structure of the soil and return nitrogen to the lawn.

The shorter the clippings, the more easily they fall to the soil (as opposed to lying on top of the grass), and the more quickly they decompose. Optimally, you should never cut more than one-third off the total height of the grass. This means you may need to mow your lawn on a slightly more frequent schedule, but it's a small price to pay for improving the health of your lawn while eliminating the effort involved in bagging and hauling clippings away.

Step 2: Use a fertilizer with a nitrogen component that comes from a natural source, or urea form, both of which release nitrogen slowly. Other forms of nitrogen may provide a quick green-up, but they are so highly soluble that much of the nitrogen leaches through to the soil without the grass ever having a chance to use it. These soluble forms of nitrogen, such as ammonium nitrate, have caused problems by polluting groundwater and nearby streams and lakes.

Step 3: Relax your standards somewhat regarding what you consider to be weeds. No less than the great American horticulturist, Liberty Hyde Bailey, wrote in 1898: "The man who worries morning and night about dandelions in the lawn will find great relief in loving the dandelions. Each blossom is worth more than a gold coin, as it shimmers in exuberant sunlight of the growing spring, and attracts the bees to its bosom. Little children love the dandelions: why not we? Love the things nearest at hand; and love intensely."

Instead of trying to achieve that nearly impossible perfect grass lawn, completely free of dandelions, crabgrass, clover and whatnot, why not leave the herbicides on the shelf and simply mow what you've got? A lawn with a few weeds in it is not going to stop anyone from having a grand time playing touch football, badminton or hide-and-seek. Leave perfection to the greenskeepers and their putting greens.

Step 4: Finally, if insect pests become a serious problem, opt for a natural control. Great strides have been made in the science of organic pesticides. Today there is an effective, natural control product available for every lawn pest. These products make sense not only from an environmental point of view, but from a personal one as well. All you have to do is imagine the number of times kids fall face down in the grass during an active game of volleyball or football, or just how close babies or toddlers are to the lawn as they crawl or wobble across the grass, and the choice of insect remedies becomes clear-cut.

A well-maintained lawn is the near perfect complement to a well-maintained house. Note that "well-maintained" need not mean "perfect."

HOBBY GARDENS

The best thing about a landscape planted with low-maintenance plantings is that it leaves you free to pursue other interests. Ironically, one of those other interests may be gardening. If you're scratching your head right now, that statement is not meant to be a conundrum. It's just that a big yard, full of high-maintenance plantings, is simply overwhelming to many people. But when high-maintenance plantings are restricted to a small, separate, defined area, they're much easier to manage. Their upkeep becomes a leisure-time hobby rather than a demanding, regular chore.

Most hobbies, of any sort, have many dimensions. That's what makes a hobby interesting and worth pursuing. The five types of gardens featured on pages 86 through 98—water gardens, kitchen gardens, herb gardens, cutting gardens and rose gardens—fall easily into the hobby category. Each has a long, rich history and provides unique plants for use in a variety of crafts and activities beyond the garden.

Planting flowers to attract butterflies can bring an amazing amount of life to the garden.

The other two types of gardens—the wildlife sanctuary (pages 100-101) and the wildflower garden (pages 102-105)—are birds of a different feather, with plenty of room for personal interpretation. With all of these specialty gardens the rewards are disproportionate to the space you can devote to them: no matter how small they may be in square feet, your enjoyment and satisfaction can be great.

A wildflower garden can be measured in acres or in square feet; either way, you'll love it and so will the birds, bees and butterflies.

Hobby gardening is about having fun with plants, rather than hard work. The secret is to keep the scale of your gardening reasonable.

Above Right: Gardening in containers is extremely satisfying and the size of the garden can be easily expanded or contracted.

Left: One of the most satisfying and low-maintenance forms of gardening is water gardening.

WATER GARDENS

Florence Yoch, the brilliant landscape architect quoted earlier, had this to say about water: "Water is always essential and is by far the most interesting feature in any garden."

Although it has been many years since a fountain or pool was considered a garden essential, it has become the fastest-growing type of gardening in America today. Because of its increasing popularity,

water gardening now offers a wide variety of options, and they are more widely available than at any time in the past.

Fountains and ponds are the most common ways of adding water to a landscape, but even something as simple as a birdbath adds a little of water's reflective charm to the garden, while at the same time doing something nice for the birds.

Another simple way to add water in a garden setting, though seldom seen anymore, is with a dipping well. Dipping wells must be filled from a hose, but what they lack in practicality they make up for in charm. Anything like an old well-head, a large porcelain pot, a stone or cast-concrete trough or a large rock with a hollowed-out basin to hold the water can be used as a dipping well. With a long-handled dipper nearby, you can use the dipping well for watering container plants and as a place to wash off your hands or bare feet. Birds undoubtedly will find their way to the dipping well and will thank you for your thoughtfulness with frequent patronage.

If you decide on a fountain or pool, the type you choose is largely a matter of personal preference and the opportunities afforded by your yard.

Wonderful terra-cotta and pre-cast wall fountains come complete

Considering the relative ease with which they can be installed, water gardens provide a wealth of pleasures in return.

Many gardeners take extreme care when choosing stones for their water gardens, hand-picking each one.

with recirculating pumps. Rigid fiberglass liners, which are available in many shapes and depths, make installing a pool almost as easy as digging a hole. Heavy, long-lasting rubber liners are available for custom-shaped pools. And although few people go to the expense and trouble anymore, there's always the option of a garden pool formed from poured concrete. There are few hard-and-fast rules regarding fountain and pool styles, with the exception that formal (geometrically shaped) pools look best in formal gardens and pools and waterfalls of natural (free-form) designs are best suited to informal yards.

Whatever you choose, take advantage of water's magnetic charms and place a fountain in an alluring location—one that can be readily seen or glimpsed from the house. Fountains make wonderful eye-catchers at the far end of a view across a garden, sure to inspire visitors to walk the full length of your yard.

If you want to grow water plants, including any of the wonderful water lilies or lotuses, locate the pool where it will receive at least 6 hours of sunlight a day. Choose a level location, one out of the path of run-off from rain and sprinklers and one that doesn't collect leaves in the fall.

Natural-looking, free-form pools lend themselves well to natural plantings around the edges. Catalogs that specialize in water gardening have recently begun stocking a good selections of bog plants, which are re-

ally quite unlike any other plants normally seen in most gardens. Whether you choose a gunnera plant (which grows up to 8 feet tall with leaves between 4 and 8 feet across), papyrus (with its tall, skinny stems and umbrella-like foliage) or any of the other exotic bog-loving plants, they're sure to inspire comment.

In addition to the spectacular hardy and tropical-flowering wa-

terlilies and lotus, there are many varieties of iris which bloom magnificently with "wet feet," including Japanese, Louisiana and Siberian types. Other popular water and bog plants include various rushes, Sagittaria, parrot's feather, primrose creeper, cattails, cannas, arrowhead and many varieties of taro.

All plants grown directly in the pond, underwater, are planted in

Water gardening allows for a delightful combination of textures, colors, sights and sounds.

Water gardening not only delights the eye and ear, but opens up a whole new world of unusual aquatic plants with which to experiment.

containers filled with a heavy soil mix. The depth underwater can be adjusted using one or more layers of bricks under each container. Plant bog plants around the edge of the pond, either in containers sunk into the ground or directly in the soil. Many gardeners prefer planting bog plants in containers to help control their aggressive habits.

Water gardens are rewarding in many ways. The most rewarding may be the magical way they bring a garden to life, inviting even the most harried and preoccupied person to sit a moment and reflect at the water's edge. Although it may seem like an extravagant extra, give serious consideration to adding a water garden in your yard. You may not get around to constructing it this year or next, but when you do, you'll have only one regret— that you didn't build it sooner.

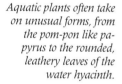

Aquatic plants often take on unusual forms, from the pom-pon like papyrus to the rounded, leathery leaves of the water hyacinth.

Not all water gardens need to be installed below ground: Here, a "raised bed" approach was taken with the help of a black plastic liner and wide boards for sides.

Aside from the occasional removal of leaves and other debris, there's not much a water garden demands in the way of maintenance.

FISH FOR YOUR POND

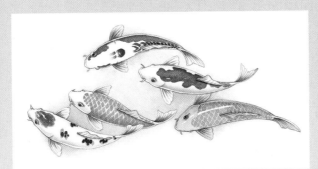

Goldfish and their larger cousins, koi, are natural inhabitants of water gardens, adding an exotic shimmer of life and color beneath the water's surface. Pond owners are quick to tell you of the joys of maintaining goldfish or koi—how responsive they are at feeding time, how little care they need and the thrill of presiding over a batch of baby fish. In areas where raccoons are prevalent, you may have to take some precautions against their using your pool as a fishing hole. Both goldfish and koi live for decades and can dwell year-round in your pool, even in cold-winter climates, provided the pool is outfitted with a simple electric pool heater. Goldfish and koi are normally fed once or twice a day—just the amount they will eat in 3 minutes or so—and only during temperate weather.

As weather turns cold and the water temperature in your pond drops below 50°F, the fish will go dormant and no feeding will be necessary until the water warms again. Pet stores and water garden catalogs sell specially formulated fish food for goldfish and koi.

INSTALLING A RIGID LINER POND

1 Set the liner where you want it to go and mark the outside perimeter on the ground using a sharp stick or screwdriver.

2 Mark the high and low spots of the pond and excavate the hole accordingly.

3 Set the pond in place, making sure it is well-supported from the bottom. Fill in low spots with sand, if necessary.

4 Start filling the pond with water and use a level to make sure the top edge is level–otherwise, the water in your pool will be "lop-sided."

5 As a final touch, cover the rim of the pool with flat rocks to make it look more natural and incorporate it into the garden. Once the rocks are in place, it's time for any plants you may want to add around the edge of the pool.

Peppers—from the hottest to the mildest— are well-behaved plants that produce a surprisingly large crop. Shown here: 'Hungarian' sweet peppers.

Left: Kitchen gardens can trace their history back to the monastic gardens of medieval times, and often retain some of that ancient formality.

KITCHEN GARDENS

If you enjoy cooking, there's nothing quite so satisfying as being able to step out your back door to grab that bit of parsley or basil you need for a pot of simmering soup, pick a few of your favorite hot peppers to spice up a salsa, or bite into that first eagerly awaited, vine-ripened tomato. While the old-fashioned, rambling vegetable garden may be hard to fit into most of today's smaller backyards—not to mention hard to fit into your schedule—a small kitchen garden of herbs, vegetables and flowers can easily fit into almost any backyard and be a delight, rather than a pain, to maintain.

Kitchen gardens (or as the French call them, potagers) are directly related to the cloistered gardens in medieval monasteries. In essence, the cloistered garden was a garden

of choice, useful plants, located close at hand, given special attention and protected by the cloister walls. The plants included many herbs, a few vegetables and a variety of flower-

Any kitchen garden—no matter what its size—should make room for both vegetables and flowers. Shown here, a combination of zinnias and cabbage.

ing plants used for medicinal purposes. Because of the interesting combination of plants, and the fact that they received close, daily attention (some might say devotion), these were attractive small plots, admired as much for their beauty as for their culinary contributions.

Today's kitchen gardens have retained their artful/edible split personality. Typically laid out in a square planting bed, say 10 feet by 10 feet, kitchen gardens are often four neatly edged symmetrical beds (each 60 inches square), filled with vegetables, herbs and a few flowers, and designed and planted with an eye toward beauty as well as produce for the kitchen table.

Neat patterns of different-colored lettuces create a tapestry effect, green onion tops march in military precision, and four string-bean-covered teepees mark the outside corners of the garden.

As a crowning touch, a sundial, birdbath or gazing ball may be placed in the center of the garden, perhaps surrounded by those heavenly blue flowers of the borage plant and orange nasturtiums. (The flowers of both are edible and make wonderful additions to salads.)

Plant your kitchen garden as close to the kitchen as possible, in a spot where it will receive at least 6 hours of sunlight each day. Limit the vegetables and herbs to those that you really enjoy using on a regular basis, and, whenever possible, plant dwarf or compact varieties of standard vegetables for the most efficient use of space.

Although your list may differ, the following are some favorite kitchen garden candidates: peas, radishes, scallions, beets, broccoli, fennel, lettuce, bush beans, cucumbers, eggplants, peppers, squash and tomatoes. As far as herbs go, most good cooks consider parsley, basil, chives, dill, thyme, sage and tarragon indispensable.

If there's no room to plant a kitchen garden, even the smallest of decks or patios can support a good variety of vegetables grown in containers—as long as the spot receives at least 6 hours of sun and you're willing to be diligent in your watering practices.

All types of peppers, tomatoes, bush forms of squash, cucumbers, eggplants and any type of herb perform admirably in containers. For the best results, choose the largest containers possible, filled with a lightweight, packaged soil mix (not soil from the garden). After planting vegetable transplants in the containers, feed with a pelleted, slow-release fertilizer according to package directions. You may have to use some stakes, trellises and ties to keep your miniature kitchen garden tidy, but you'll be surprised at the amount of fresh vegetables it will produce.

If you want to make it easy on yourself, consider creating a kitchen garden out of a series of raised beds filled with top-quality soil.

Because of their compact plant habit, eggplants make a great addition to a small kitchen garden. Shown here: 'Morden Midget'.

Sometimes the division between "ornamental" and "edible" becomes blurred with kitchen gardens.

Harking back to their medieval monastic origins, many contemporary kitchen gardens have retained a formal, geometric style.

HERB GARDENS

More than a few people with only a passing interest in cooking or gardening have found themselves fascinated with growing and using herbs. That fascination is not all that surprising, because, as a group, herbs may well be the most intriguing of all plants to grow. Complementing their unique flavors, virtually all herbs grown today have their own complex history and a fascinating legacy of folklore. Start with a single parsley plant, and in a couple of sea-

Chamomile, like lavender, is as beautiful as it is useful.

sons you may find yourself hooked on growing every type of herb you can find.

It's easy to create a small herb garden, and very rewarding too. A space as small as a 5- by 5-foot plot is ample for a good sampling of herbs. Many popular herbs are from the sunny Mediterranean region and grow naturally in gravelly, lean soil. Make sure your herb plants feel right at home by locating the bed in a full-sun location and filling it with a fast-draining soil. If the

soil is naturally heavy, add a few bags of organic soil amendment (such as compost or leaf mold) to the plot and turn it into the top 6 or 8 inches of soil. Add fertilizer sparingly, if at all.

It's a good idea to label the herb plants to help those who might be unfamiliar with what herbs look like—such as young children—should they ever be sent out to the garden to gather a little of this or that for the evening meal.

You can plant the herbs in whatever arrangement pleases you, formal or informal. Some gardeners take special enjoyment from planting intricate, living patterns with their herb plants, using dwarf, small-leaved basil plants to create fast-growing green boundaries between the various herbs, much like a little clipped boxwood hedge.

DRYING YOUR HERBS

One of the best things about an herb garden is that you can enjoy its bounty year-round. Any herb can be

dried, and as long as it is kept in a cool, dry, dark location, its flavor and pungency will remain intact for 6 months or more.

Toward the end of the growing season, your herb plants will have grown so large that it will be possible to harvest

Drying herbs.

large amounts for drying and still have enough left in the garden for fresh use.

The easiest way to dry herbs is simply to cut the branches about 9 to 12 inches long and gather them together in small bundles. Tie the ends together with a piece of sting and hang upside down in a warm, dry place, preferably out of direct sunlight. Most herbs will be completely dry in 5 to 7 days.

Once dry, strip the leaves from the branches and store in clean, dry glass jars, preferably dark-colored ones, which keep sunlight from diminishing their flavor. Cover tightly and store in a cool place.

WINDOW BOX HERBS

If space is at a premium, you can still enjoy the benefits of fresh herbs in a window box, especially attractive and practical when placed under the kitchen window. Be aware from the beginning that window boxes are not low-maintenance: their limited space and intense planting demand regular attention, especially with watering; during warm weather, it's not unusual for window boxes to need daily waterings.

If possible, favor dwarf forms of herbs, if available, such as 'Spicy Globe' basil, or naturally diminutive types, like any of the various thymes. Thyme, and the prostrate (or hanging) form of rosemary are attractive for their ability to spill over the edges of the window box. Avoid large, rank-growing herbs, such as dill and borage, which will lend an unkempt look to the planting.

"MUST-HAVE" HERBS FOR COOKS

Basil. The small-leaved varieties, such as 'Basilico Greco', 'Spicy Globe' and 'Piccolo Verde Fino' are all as ornamental as they are flavorful.

Chives.

Chives. Standard chives, with their thin, round stems and pink blossoms, and their close cousins, garlic chives, with a pronounced garlic flavor and flat leaves, are both beautiful and flavorful. Both the leaves and the flowers are edible. Both make great edging plants in the herb garden.

Cilantro. This is an herb you either love or hate; there's no in-between. If you love it, you probably can't get enough of it. Cilantro prefers cool weather and most varieties are quick to go to seed once warm weather and long days arrive. Look for the variety 'Slobolt' to avoid this problem.

Dill.

Dill. The distinctive flavor of dill is essential for many canning recipes and a wonderful complement to vegetables (such as carrots and new potatoes) and all types of fresh fish. Standard varieties will grow to 5 feet or more tall; compact varieties such as 'Dukat' or 'Tetra Dill' are much more compact but every bit as productive.

Oregano. Popular in many Italian, Greek and Mexican recipes, oregano is very easy to grow. Makes a nice edging plant in the herb garden.

Parsley. It's hard to have too much parsley. The flat-leaved Italian parsley is favored by chefs for its intense flavor, while the curly-leafed types are popular for garnishes and cooking.

Sage. Even if it didn't have such a characteristic flavor, sage would be planted in gardens for its ornamental value. There are many varieties—from variegated to purple-leafed—and they combine beautifully in one planting. A favorite complement to sausage, stuffing and pork.

Tarragon. With its elusive anise flavor, tarragon is highly regarded by French cooks for a variety of dishes and sauces. True French tarragon does not grow true from seed, so if you want the real thing, you'll have to buy it as a transplant from your local nursery or mail-order herb catalog.

Thyme.

Thyme. The many varieties of thyme are as ornamental as they are flavorful. An essential flavor in many French and Italian dishes. Favor the standard thyme for cooking, such as 'French' summer thyme, and then branch out to some of the more exotic types, such as lemon thyme.

There's nothing quite like the luxury of having an abundance of flowers for cutting—right outside your back door.

CUTTING GARDENS

Many people who have flowers growing in their yards are reluctant to cut them, for fear that they'll diminish the beauty on display. If you like cut flowers, the easiest way to ensure a ready supply for arrangements—without denuding the border next to the lawn—is to plant a cutting garden. It's a rather old-fashioned notion, but one well worth reviving.

Think of a cutting garden as a utilitarian type of garden, not unlike a plot of vegetables. With the bed hidden away in a side yard, behind a fence, or in a far corner of your backyard, you're free to plant flowers in practical rows, rather than trying to create aesthetically pleasing combinations, as you might if the bed were on public display. And just as you would with a vegetable garden, make sure there are paths between the rows to permit easy maintenance and cutting.

Another benefit of creating a special cutting garden is that as beautiful as the following flowers are, some of the plants they grow on tend to be either rangy and not all that well-behaved, or short-lived. By growing them in a sequestered location, their bad habits will not be so objectionable.

And there's one other bit of good news: As you read through the following descriptions of some of the top-rated flowers for cutting, notice how many are best grown from seed planted directly in the garden. Direct-sowing of seed is not only easy, it's incredibly inexpensive—especially when you compare the cost of the seed to the amount of enjoyment the flowers bring into your life.

The choice of which flowers to plant is, of course, up to you, but plant at least some annuals. They come into flower quickly after planting, have a long blooming season and, best of all, the more you cut them the more they bloom. Many annuals are available in both dwarf and standard forms; the standard or tall forms will provide the longest stems for cutting.

GREAT CUTTING GARDEN FLOWERS

Bells of Ireland (*Moluccella laevis*). This old-fashioned, all-green flower with its 2-foot-long spikes of apple green, shell-like blossoms, is particularly attractive for flower arrangers looking for the unusual. Beautiful fresh, bells of Ireland can be easily dried—and keep their color well—by hanging the stems upside down in a warm, dark, dry place. Start this summer annual from seed planted in the garden when all danger of frost has passed, in a full-sun location. Cut individual stems of bells of Ireland when at least half of the "shells" are open. If you condition the stems in warm water overnight, they'll last up to 2 weeks in an arrangement.

Chinese lantern plant (*Physalis alkekengi*), so named for the long-lasting, bright orange, papery husks that surround its fruit, is one of the most decorative of all garden plants. Very easy to grow from seed, be aware that the Chinese lantern plant's long underground stems can become invasive, especially in mild-winter climates. Sow seed of this perennial (usually grown as an annual) directly in a loose soil in spring in a full-sun location. It is relatively drought resistant, but will produce larger "lanterns" if watered regularly. Cut branches when the husks have turned a deep, bright orange. Stems dry on their own (without hanging upside down) without any loss of color. If carefully stored, stems can be kept from year to year.

Cornflower (*Centaurea cyanus*). Few sights are as charming as a bunch of blue cornflowers in a simple white vase. While best known (and loved) for their intense blue color, cornflowers (also known as bachelor's buttons) come in shades of white, pink, rose, wine and bicolors. Depending on the variety, plants grow from 1 to 2¹/2 feet tall; all make wonderful cut flowers. Cornflowers are very easy to grow, but because they don't like to be transplanted, sow seeds directly onto ordinary garden soil in late fall or early spring. Cornflowers do best in a sunny location. Although an annual, cornflowers reseed readily; once they're planted, you'll probably continue to have volunteer cornflowers in your garden in succeeding years. Cut anytime flowers are in bloom. Strip foliage from lower stems. For maximum blossoms, remove faded flowers from plants.

Canterbury bells (*Campanula medium*), with stems, up to 4 feet tall, covered with cup-and-saucer-shaped flowers in shades of pink, blue and white, make a dramatic statement both in the garden and in arrangements. Plant nursery-grown transplants in the garden in early spring in a loose, well-drained soil. Plant in full sun or partial shade and keep soil evenly moist. Once blooms appear, stake to keep the top-heavy flowers from tumbling.

Chrysanthemum (*Dendranthema grandiflorum*). This so-called "florists' chrysanthemum" is the most useful mum for home cutting gardens and the undisputed king of the fall flower garden. Plants range in height from 2 to 4 feet tall. Plant rooted cuttings in early spring in a loose, well-drained, fertile soil in a sunny location. Allow 1¹/2 to 2 feet between each plant. For maximum flowers and minimum staking, pinch plants back twice: once when they are about 8 inches tall and again when the resulting new growth has grown an additional 6 inches; leave at least two leaves per stem. To give flower buds enough time to form, do not pinch stems after the middle of July. Even with conscientious pinching, some of the taller mums will need to be staked. Keep plants consistently watered. If you want the largest possible flowers, remove all but one flower bud per stem. Cut stems of chrysanthemums when the flowers are almost completely open. If the stems are woody, use a sharp knife to split them vertically an inch or so. Strip off the lower leaves on each stem. In addition to their great beauty, chrysanthemums are among the longest lasting of all cut flowers, often lasting up to 3 weeks with frequent changes of water.

Dahlias (*Dahlia* hybrids). Available in a wide variety of vibrant colors and flower forms, dahlias make wonderful cut flowers. The dinner-plate-sized dahlias favored a generation or so ago have been superseded by smaller, easier-to-arrange varieties. Plant sizes range from 1¹/2 to over 6 feet tall. As an added bonus, dahlias continue to bloom prolifically right up to the first frost, often rivaling chrysanthemums in their autumn beauty. Dahlias are considered perennials, even though they are grown from tubers. The already-started plants available in spring are fine for bed and border displays; plant dormant tubers for the best cutting flowers.

Great Cutting Garden Flowers Continued...

Gloriosa daisy (*Rudbeckia hirta*). With its stiff stems and glorious summer colors, the gloriosa daisy is one of the best of all cut flowers. Also known as black-eyed Susan, this short-lived perennial is usually grown as an annual. Gloriosa daisies bloom prolifically over a long season. With their increased popularity, several named varieties have been introduced, including one with green centers called "Irish Eyes." True to their native wildflower roots, gloriosa daisies are very easy to grow. Plant transplants in the early spring, or plant seeds directly in average garden soil after the last spring frost, in a full-sun location. Cut gloriosa daisies as soon as the flowers are completely open. If you change the water daily, gloriosa daisies will last a week or more in an arrangement.

Larkspur (*Consolida ambigua*). This old-fashioned favorite deserves wider popularity, particularly for flower arrangers. Larkspur is also known as annual delphinium, which it resembles. Available in shades of white, blue, lilac, pink, rose, coral and wine, larkspur grows from 1 to 5 feet tall, depending on the variety. Best grown from seed sown directly in an average garden soil, preferably in the fall for bloom the following spring. Plant in a full-sun location. Wait until at least half the flowers on the spike have opened before cutting larkspur.

Lisianthus (*Eustoma grandiflorum*). A relative newcomer to the home garden, lisianthus hybrids produce flowers that look almost like roses, in shades of white, lavender blue and pink. The 18-inch-tall plants aren't much to look at, but the flowers are stunning and have quickly become a favorite with flower arrangers. Best grown from nursery-grown transplants. Plant in a loose, well-drained soil in a full-sun location. Keep plants consistently watered and feed once a month with an all-purpose fertilizer for best blooms. Cut lisianthus when flowers are almost completely open. The thin, wire-like stems are much sturdier than they look, perfect for flower arranging. Very long lasting as a cut flower, especially if the water is changed frequently.

Love-in-a-mist (*Nigella damascena*). Popular several generations ago, love-in-a-mist is making a big comeback to home gardens. Plants grow to 2^1/2 feet tall and have very finely cut foliage. The blue, white or pink flowers have a subtle beauty. Faded flowers are replaced by papery husks valued by flower arrangers for their unusual appeal. Best bet is to grow love-in-a-mist from seed in early spring, sown directly where you want them in the garden. Plant in average garden soil in a full sun. Quick to come into bloom, love-in-a-mist declines just as quickly as summer weather warms. Will reseed readily, returning to the garden year after year. Cut love-in-a-mist when at least two flowers in a cluster are open. Strip lower foliage from stems. Stems with seed pods can be successfully dried by hanging upside down in a warm, dry place.

Mexican sunflower (*Tithonia rotundifolia*). If you haven't tried growing the Mexican sunflower, by all means do. A very willing performer, Mexican sunflower grows quickly to an astounding 6 feet tall, making it perfect for a back-of-the-border location. Heat and drought tolerant and remarkably pest- and disease-free, this plant makes few demands on the gardener. Best of all is its profusion of long-stemmed flowers: single daisy-like blossoms in the most brilliant orange red you've ever seen. Beautiful when combined with blue cornflowers. Best grown from seed sown directly in average garden soil. Plant in spring when all danger of frost has passed, in a full-sun location. Cut Mexican sunflowers when flowers are fully open. Stems are hollow, so handle carefully to avoid damage.

Shirley poppies (*Papaver rhoeas*). The scarlet red Shirley poppy, with its characteristic black center, is known throughout Europe as the Flanders field poppy. These old-fashioned favorites, with their strong, wiry stems, make wonderful cut flowers. Breeding efforts have produced many excellent named varieties that produce both single and double flowers in shades of red, pink, white, orange, coral and bicolors. Although nursery-grown transplants are available, most gardeners prefer to sow Shirley poppies from seed directly where they want them in the garden. The very fine seed can be combined with sand for easier broadcasting. Plant seed in late fall or very early spring in a well-drained soil and sunny location. Allow some of the flowers to produce seed pods; dry and shake seeds on the soil for a repeat performance next year. Cut Shirley poppies just when buds begin to show color. To prolong their vase life, immediately singe the cut ends of the stems by passing through a flame.

Sunflower (*Helianthus annuus*). Few annuals are as satisfying or as easy to grow as sunflowers. The old-fashioned, tall sunflower—typified by the 'Russian Mammoth' variety—is a stunner, but not the first choice for flower arrangers. Many newer, shorter, multi-branched varieties are available; all are prolific summer bloomers. Mainly available in sunny shades of yellow, gold and rust, some European imports are more subtle, with pale cream and butter yellow flowers. Choose a sunny location with average garden soil; sow seeds directly where you want the sunflowers to grow, after all danger of frost has passed. Although they are somewhat drought tolerant, sunflowers will perform better with regular watering. Cut sunflowers as soon as the petals have opened. Split stems vertically (an inch or so) with a sharp knife to permit better water absorption.

Sweet peas (*Lathyrus odoratus*). The haunting, sweet fragrance of sweet peas—along with their pastel colors and charming forms—have made them a favorite for countless generations of gardeners. To grow sweet peas successfully, several requirements must be met: cool weather, a loose, well-drained soil with a neutral pH, a full-sun location and, because sweet pea vines grow to 6 feet or more, some kind support for them to grow on. Virtually all gardeners start sweet peas from seed, planted very early in the spring, directly where they are to grow. For better germination, soak seeds in water for 24 hours before planting. Cut sweet peas just as they open fully. Use a commercially available floral preservative in the vase water for longer life.

Zinnias (*Zinnia elegans*). If you think you know zinnias, you may want to think again. There have been so many improvements in the world of zinnias, every cut-flower enthusiast should take a good look at a seed catalog or two just to see what's available. New flower forms, new colors (including bicolors) and new plant habits have created a lot of excitement with this common summer annual. With their sturdy stems and extensive range of colors, zinnias are among the best of all cut flowers. Zinnias are extremely easy to grow and grow well. All they require is a sunny location, plenty of heat, a loose, well-drained soil and consistent water. If you remove old, spent flowers, zinnias will bloom prolifically all summer long, right up to the first frost in fall. Nurseries and garden centers offer already-started transplants, but for the best selection and unusual varieties, start zinnias from seed. As they will not tolerate frost, wait until spring weather has thoroughly warmed, and plant zinnia seeds directly in the garden. Cut zinnias for arranging when the flowers have just fully opened.

CUTTING AND CONDITIONING FLOWERS

Of course it's possible to simply walk into the garden, cut some flowers and arrange them in a vase. But it's also disappointing to have those same flowers fade the day after the arrangement was made. The process known as "conditioning" will help any flower stay at its best for the longest possible time; if you haven't tried it before, you'll be surprised at the difference it makes.

Begin by cutting all stems at an angle; this give a larger surface area for water absorption. Remove any leaves that will be below the water level in the vase. For flowers with woody stems, cut a 1-inch-long slit at the stems' base. Stems should always be recut immediately before placing them in the water, even if you have just gathered them from the garden.

Using the deepest bucket on hand, fill it with cold water and place in the coolest, darkest spot you can find. Stand the flowers in the water (the water should come about three-quarters up the stems) and allow to sit for a minimum of 6 hours and, if possible, 24 hours.

Although there is some controversy over the best time to cut flowers from the garden, recent evidence indicates that cutting them in the middle of the day may be the best of all, and exactly the opposite of what is normally recommended. During the middle of the day (especially during periods of hot weather) the flowers will be stressed for water and will readily absorb the water you sink them into, preventing air bubbles from forming in the stems. Air bubbles in the stem are one of the main reasons for premature wilting of cut flowers. Give it a try.

ROSE GARDENS

With their great beauty, tremendous variety and luscious scent, it's easy to become passionate about those all-time favorites, roses. For many, roses are the symbol of a well-cared-for home, evoking images of that picket-fenced cottage awash with rambling roses. In addition to being beautiful flowers for arrangements, roses lend themselves to a wide variety of crafts, providing everything from petals for creating potpourri, to the vitamin C-rich seed pods (called rose hips) for rose hip tea.

To do what they do so well—namely, produce quantities of beautiful, fragrant flowers—roses need special attention. Although it's possible to mix any number of roses in with a shrub border, it's far easier to be lavish with that attention if they are segregated in a small bed. Ten to 12 rose bushes will make a magnificent display, provide plenty of flowers for cutting and require a bed only 8 feet by 12 feet or so. Any shape of bed will do, but generations of gardeners have favored the formal look of square, rectangular or round beds, edged with stone or brick, often with a birdbath or sundial placed in the center for a little added interest.

'Iceberg' rose.

From old-fashioned heirloom roses to modern-day hybrid tea varieties, there's enough variation among roses to keep anyone interested for a lifetime.

If you want maximum return on your bed of roses, four important requirements should be taken into consideration:
• selection of the rose varieties,
• location of the planting bed,
• soil preparation and
• consistent care.

When choosing roses, always favor those adapted to your growing region. Consult local gardening authorities—your neighborhood nursery, county extension agent or garden club—for a list of roses that grow well in your area. The list may not contain all (or any, for that matter) of your favorites, but there will be plenty to choose from, some of which are bound to become new favorites.

The selection process is a very important step in the creation of a successful rose garden. By choosing naturally vigorous roses, you will dramatically decrease the amount of care they require.

A small bed of roses can function as the focal point of a yard, but don't let design considerations blind you to roses' specific needs. In the main, roses require a location that's sunny at least 6 hours a day.

Ideally, the location should provide good air circulation and receive morning sun to help dry off leaves early in the day. Too much shade encourages disease problems. If the shade is produced by mature trees, their extensive root systems will rob nutrients from the roses, a situation that results in few flowers and weak plants. And if there are youngsters in your household, take care to locate the rose bed where an errant football or frisbee isn't likely to wreak havoc.

Once you have outlined the shape of the rose bed, it's time to improve the soil—before planting the roses. Because roses are rather finicky about soil, it's a good idea to have your soil tested. Some large nurseries and most university extension services will do this for a nominal charge. Once the soil analysis is complete, you will know exactly what should be added to the soil and in what amount. This is not the time for skimping. Any extra effort you put into advance preparation will pay off in superior results for years to come.

'Bonica' rose.

'Peace' rose.

Standard care includes watering, fertilizing, protecting against pests and diseases, and pruning. Roses need regular applications of water for top production of flowers. It makes no difference whether the water comes from a hose or from rain. Just make sure the roses receive enough water to moisten the soil to a depth of 18 inches every week during the growing season. The easiest way to check this is with a long screwdriver or stiff piece of wire, such as a straightened-out coat hanger. Either device will be easy to push through moist soil, more difficult once it hits dry soil. In arid summer climates, consider watering your roses with a drip system that is connected to a timer.

At least two applications of fertilizer should be made, once when new growth first starts in the spring and again in midseason. Favor non-burning, natural formulations that feed the soil as well as the plant.

Vigorously growing roses will be far less susceptible to attack from pests and diseases than those that are struggling. There are effective natural controls for virtually every pest known to plague roses. If you

'Mr. Lincoln' rose.

know of diseases that are a problem in your area (such as black spot, rust and mildew), use a natural fungicide to combat the problem before it occurs. Diseases are impossible to eradicate once they make an appearance, although they can be stopped from doing additional damage.

FAVORITE ROSES

For Fragrance: 'Chrysler Imperial', 'Double Delight', 'Fragrant Cloud', 'Fragrant Memory', 'Graham Thomas', 'Mme. Hardy', 'Mr. Lincoln', 'Pink Peace'.

For Abundant and Long Season of Bloom: 'Betty Prior', 'Escapade', 'Europeana', 'Gene Boerner', 'Iceberg', 'Margaret Merril', 'Sunsprite'.

For Cutting: 'Champney's Pink Cluster', 'Iceberg', 'Louise Odier', 'Mermaid', 'Mr. Lincoln', 'Mme. Isaac Pereire', 'Sombreuil'.

Favorite Heirloom Varieties: 'Duchesse de Brabant', 'Empress Josephine', 'Frau Karl Druschki', 'Great Maiden's Blush', 'Honorine de Brabant', 'Konigin von Danemark', 'Mme. Hardy', 'Old Blush', 'Reine des Violettes', 'Sombreuil', 'Souvenir de la Malmaison', 'Zephirine Drouhin'.

For Disease Resistance: 'Bonica', 'Bredon', 'Carefree Wonder', 'Dortmund', 'Graham Thomas', 'Max Graf', 'Stanwell Perpetual'.

WILDLIFE SANCTUARIES

The preceding hobby gardens can be confined to a small space. When it comes to converting your yard to a wildlife sanctuary, it's customary to convert the entire yard, not just one small part of it. Granted, gardening for wildlife is much different from other types of gardening, but as far as gardening for outdoor living goes, a wildlife sanctuary may be its ultimate expression: Not only are you creating a place where you, the human inhabitant of the garden, can have a comfortable place to live outdoors, but you're also creating a space for all creatures, great and small, to enjoy as well.

While other gardeners dream about planting a rose or vegetable garden, wildlife gardeners have visions of "butterfly gardens" or "winter bird gardens." This shift in emphasis produces gardens quite unlike anything you might expect in anyone's backyard—especially in the city or suburbs.

Black-tailed jackrabbit.

You may be wondering if it's really possible to create a miniature wildlife sanctuary in an urban or a suburban backyard. The boundaries that homeowners put up around their yards don't mean a thing to most wildlife. To the bluebird or monarch butterfly flying overhead, the turtle plodding his way through the grass or the salamander slinking her way through the damp undergrowth, a backyard can simply be another bit of the environment in which they live. The reason you don't see more wildlife in backyards is that most people don't plant anything to attract wild creatures or create places for them to seek shelter. Once you do, you'll be amazed at how quickly wild creatures will

visit and at how many will take up permanent residence in your backyard.

Home wildlife gardens can be beautiful, intriguing places. In most cases, the lawns have been eliminated. Gone, too, are the neatly trimmed shrub borders, replaced with informal plantings of annuals, perennials, shrubs and trees attractive to wildlife. A meandering path covered with pine needles or bark may lead through this wonderland, past a pond or pool: a source of fresh water is essential to all forms of wildlife.

Owners of these gardens speak of them as acting like magnets. You, too, will find that the sights and sounds of wildlife, as they dive and flit about the garden, will pull you from your bed early enough for a morning stroll, even on those hurly-burly workdays. Sunlight streaming through at long angles, turning dewdrops on spider webs into diamond necklaces, the whirring of the first hummingbird as it looks for a fresh flower, the languid move-

Mr. Toad hides in the dandelions.

Butterflies love open, flat flowers, like this zinnia, to use as "landing pads."

ment of butterflies as they warm their wings in the morning sunlight and the plop of a frog as it jumps into the murky water all work in concert, creating a marvelous grace note on which to start the day.

While all gardens require upkeep, an informal garden planted with attracting wildlife in mind is far less demanding than a more traditional landscape. Plants can be allowed to find their natural forms instead of being trimmed into tidy shapes. A weed here or there isn't such an eyesore when it is growing amid a profusion of billowing plants. And if you choose to eliminate the lawn (which is not a prerequisite), one major source of upkeep is also eliminated.

Even though a wildlife garden may be informal, be sure to define places to sit, relax and take in the sights of your sanctuary. A wooden bench under a spreading tree, a couple of chaise longues on a patio overlooking the pond or a clearing in a grove of trees for a picnic table and benches will provide human comfort while you view your own private wildlife preserve.

Plants to Attract Birds

Lilies, with their colorful and tube-shaped flowers, do a good job attracting hummingbirds.

Plants to Attract Birds in the Northeast & Midwest

Brambles (*Rubus*)
Dogwood (*Cornus*)
Elderberry
  (*Sambucus canadensis*)
Honeysuckle (*Lonicera*)
Mulberry
  (*Morus alba* and *M. rubra*)
Viburnum (*Viburnum*)
Wild grapes (*Vitis lambrusca*)

Plants to Attract Birds in the Southwest

Blue elderberry
  (*Sambucus caerulea*)
Dwarf mountain ash
  (*Sorbus scopulina*)
Shrub live oak
  (*Quercus turbinella*)
Squawbush sumac
  (*Rhus trilobata*)
Utah honeysuckle
  (*Lonicera utahensis*)
Utah juniper
  (*Juniperus osteosperma*)
Utah serviceberry
  (*Amelanchier utahensis*)

Plants to Attract Birds in the South & Southeast

American beautyberry
  (*Callicarpa*)
Blackberry (*Rubus*)
Black cherry (*Prunus serotina*)
Blueberry (*Vaccinium ashei*)
Cherry laurel
  (*Prunus caroliniana*)
Dogwood (*Cornus*)
Elderberry (*Sambucus*)
Florida trema
  (*Trema guineensis*)
Pokeweed
  (*Phytolacca americana*)
Privet (*Ligustrum*)
Red mulberry (*Morus rubra*)
Sassafras (*Sassafras albidum*)
Spicebush (*Calycanthus*)
Viburnum (*Viburnum*)
Wax myrtle (*Myrica cerifera*)

Plants to Attract Birds in the Pacific Northwest

Blueberries
  (*Vaccinium angustifolium*)
Currants (*Ribes*)
Mahonia (*Mahonia*)
Mountain ash (*Sorbus*)
Native huckleberries
  (*Vaccinium*)
Salal (*Gaultheria shallon*)
Serviceberry
  (*Amelanchier alnifolia*)
Winterberry (*Ilex verticillata*)

Plants That Attract Hummingbirds

Althaea (*Hibiscus syriacus*)
Butterfly bush (*Buddleia*)
Canna (*Canna*)
Cardinal flower
  (*Lobelia cardinalis*)
Clematis (*Clematis*)
Columbine (*Aquilegia*)
Coral bells (*Heuchera*)
Fuchsia (*Fuchsia*)
Hibiscus
  (*Hibiscus rosa-sinensis*)
Hollyhock (*Alcea*)
Honeysuckle (*Lonicera*)
Lilac (*Syringa*)
Lily (*Lilium*)
Morning glory (*Ipomoea*)

Plants That Attract Butterflies

Aster (*Aster novae-angliae*)
Butterfly bush (*Buddleia*)
Butterfly weed (*Asclepias*)
Catnip (*Nepeta cataria*)
Goldenrod (*Solidago*)
Heliotrope
  (*Heliotropium arborescens*)
Joe Pye weed (*Eupatorium*)
Lantana (*Lantana*)
Mexican sunflower
  (*Tithonia rotundifolia*)
Purple coneflower
  (*Echinacea purpurea*)
Red valerian
  (*Centranthus ruber*)
Scarlet sage
  (*Salvia splendens*)
Stonecrop (*Sedum*)
Zinnia (*Zinnia elegans*)

Gardening with Wildlife

Since 1973, The National Wildlife Federation in Washington, D.C., has been making information available to homeowners interested in attracting wildlife to their gardens. Initial response was so strong that the federation actually created a do-it-yourself kit available to anyone interested in the subject. The Gardening With Wildlife Kit, which contains everything you need to plan a backyard wildlife habitat, can be ordered from The National Wildlife Federation, 1400 16th Street N.W., Washington, D.C. 20036-2266.

As an additional incentive, The National Wildlife Federation will, on request, certify your garden. Upon certification, the federation will send you a certificate proclaiming your yard to be an official Backyard Wildlife Habitat of the National Wildlife Federation. Why not be the first one on your block to display this certificate?

If there are youngsters in your household, this type of activity is one of the best ways to teach them the value of protecting and nurturing the environment. It's a project the whole family can benefit from, on a scale where results are almost immediate.

Whether it's a huge swath of wildflowers serving as a beautiful buffer between the house and the forest (above), or a small patch of native beauties right outside the door (inset), wildflowers are amazingly adaptable plants.

WILDFLOWER GARDENS

When most people think of wildflowers, they see them as suitable only for large plantings—plantings measured in acres instead of square feet. Nothing could be further from the truth. Wildflowers are a great, low-maintenance addition to yards of any size, whether the wildflowers are planted in traditional borders, in that rough area "out back," or as a replacement for a grass lawn.

Wildflower experts agree that the time when wildflowers are in their glory—in spring and summer—really isn't the best time to plant them. While it's certainly possible to have a successful wildflower garden by planting the seeds in spring, you simply increase your chances for success by planting in the fall.

By planting in the fall, home gardeners take advantage of a cycle that naturally takes place in the wild. Native wildflowers bloom and set seed in the spring and autumn. The seed falls to ground, or is spread from one location to another by birds and other animals. As the days grow shorter, temperatures drop, and winter's rain or snow arrives. The seed lies dormant through the winter, snug in the soil, just waiting to sprout during the first longer, warmer days of spring.

There's something unique about the beauty of wildflowers, unmatched by more "cultivated" flowers. Wildflowers have a natural, casual beauty that goes straight to the heart of gardening and they fit easily into suburban surroundings. And as a bonus, free-flowering wildflowers make great cut flowers for surprisingly long-lasting bouquets.

Unfortunately, a fair amount of misinformation regarding wildflowers has made its way into print. For the greatest success with wildflowers, heed the following advice:

- Make sure the wildflower mix you buy is either specially formulated for your geographic region, or for specific conditions, such as dry or shady locations.

- Be a comparison shopper. Find out what wildflower varieties are in a mix and how many ounces of actual wildflower seed is contained in the package—and then compare costs. Some packagers bulk up their mixes with a disproportionate amount of clover or other common seed.

- In the high-rainfall areas of the Midwest, a seed mix should contain a high proportion of perennial wildflowers. With warm spring and summer temperatures and high rainfall, plant growth is rapid in these regions and perennial species tend to naturally dominate the landscape. If you live in the Far West or Southwest, the arid summer conditions there require different mixes, with an emphasis on annual varieties—ones which reseed readily, from one year to the next.

- If at all possible, plant wildflower seeds in the fall. Although they can be planted in the early spring, fall-planted wildflowers perform much better because the gardener is working in harmony with the natural rhythm of nature.

- Take the time to properly prepare the soil before planting the seed. This idea, combined with purchasing the best quality seed for your area, virtually ensures the success of any wildflower planting.

Proper soil preparation starts with removing—either by hand, tilling or the use of a biodegradable herbicide such as glyphosate (sold commercially as Round-up or Kleen-up)—all weeds from the planting bed. Till the soil lightly, and if no rains are expected, irrigate the bed for a few days, for 20 minutes or so each day.

A new crop of weeds will sprout, encouraged by the tilling and irrigation. Wait until the weeds are 2 or 3 inches tall, and then make another application of glyphosate. Once the weeds have died, plant the wildflowers according to the package directions.

The combination of a little research and a little advance soil preparation will result in a stunning display of wildflowers next spring, no matter where you plant them. Be advised, however, that wildflowers can be habit-forming. More than one backyard wildflower meadow planting had its beginnings as a small border next to the lawn.

Wildflowers (right and above) have a natural charm that's hard to resist. Somewhat surprisingly, most make excellent, long-lasting cut flowers.

BEST WILDFLOWERS BY REGION

*The Mexican hat (*Ratibida columnaris) *is just one of the many wildflowers content to grow over most parts of the country.*

Wildflowers for the Northeast

Baby's breath (*Gypsophila muralis*)
Black-eyed Susan (*Rudbeckia hirta*)
Blanket flower (*Gaillardia aristata*)
Blue flax (*Linum lewisii*)
Catchfly (*Silene armeria*)
Cornflower (*Centaurea cyanus*)
Corn poppy (*Papaver rhoeas*)
Dame's rocket (*Hesperis matronalis*)
Evening primrose (*Oenothera lamarchiana*)
Foxglove (*Digitalis pupurea*)
Indian blanket (*Gaillardia pulchella*)
Northeast aster (*Aster novae-angliae*)
Perennial lupine (*Lupinus perennis*)
Plains coreopsis/calliopsis (*Coreopsis tinctoria*)
Purple coneflower (*Echinacea purpurea*)
Rocket larkspur (*Delphinium ajacus*)
Scarlet flax (*Linum rubrum*)
Shasta daisy (*Chrysanthemum maximum*)
Tickseed (*Coreopsis lanceolata*)
Wallflower (*Cheiranthus allionii*)
Yarrow (*Achillea millefolium*)

Wildflowers for the North Central States

Baby's breath (*Gypsophila muralis*)
Black-eyed Susan (*Rudbeckia hirta*)
Blanket flower (*Gaillardia aristata*)
Catchfly (*Silene armeria*)
Clasping coneflower (*Rudbeckia amplexicaulis*)
Cornflower (*Centaurea cyanus*)
Corn poppy (*Papaver rhoeas*)
Dame's rocket (*Hesperis matronalis*)
Evening primrose (*Oenothera lamarchiana*)
Indian blanket (*Gaillardia pulchella*)
Lemon mint (*Monarda citriodora*)
Mexican hat (*Ratibida columnaris*)
Missouri primrose (*Oenothera missouriensis*)
Perennial lupine (*Lupinus perennis*)
Plains coreopsis (*Coreopsis tinctoria*)
Purple coneflower (*Echinacea purpurea*)
Purple prairie clover (*Petalostemum purpureum*)
Rocket larkspur (*Delphinium ajacis*)
Scarlet flax (*Linum rubrum*)
Tahoka daisy (*Machaeranthera tanacetifolia*)
Tickseed (*Coreopsis lanceolata*)
Toadflax (*Linaria maroccana*)
Yarrow (*Achillea millefolium*)

Wildflowers for the Southeast

African daisy (*Dimorphotheca aurantica*)
Black-eyed Susan (*Rudbeckia hirta*)
Clasping coneflower (*Rudbeckia amplexicaulis*)
Cornflower (*Centaurea cyanus*)
Corn poppy (*Papaver rhoeas*)
Cosmos (*Cosmos bipinnatus*)
Dame's rocket (*Hesperis matronalis*)
Drummond phlox (*Phlox drummondii*)
Dwarf red plains coreopsis (*Coreopsis tinctoria*)
Evening primrose (*Oenothera lamarchiana*)
Five spot (*Nemophila maculata*)
Indian blanket (*Gaillardia pulchella*)
Lemon mint (*Monarda citriodora*)
Mexican hat (*Ratibida columnaris*)
Moss verbena (*Verbena tenuisecta*)
Plains coreopsis (*Coreopsis tinctoria*)
Purple coneflower (*Echinacea purpurea*)
Rocket larkspur (*Delphinium ajacis*)
Scarlet flax (*Linum rubrum*)
Showy primrose (*Oenothera speciosa*)
Sweet alyssum (*Lobularia maritima*)
Tickseed (*Coreopsis lanceolata*)
Toadflax (*Linaria maroccana*)
Yarrow (*Achillea millefolium*)

Wildflowers for the Rocky Mountain States

Black-eyed Susan (*Rudbeckia hirta*)
Blanket flower (*Gaillardia aristata*)
Blue flax (*Linum lewisii*)
Catchfly (*Silene armeria*)
Clasping coneflower (*Rudbeckia amplexicaulis*)
Cornflower (*Centaurea cyanus*)
Corn poppy (*Papaver rhoeas*)
Dame's rocket (*Hesperis matronalis*)
Evening primrose (*Oenothera lamarchiana*)
Indian blanket (*Gaillardia pulchella*)
Mexican hat (*Ratibida columnaris*)
Perennial lupine (*Lupinus perennis*)
Rocket larkspur (*Delphinium ajacis*)
Rocky Mountain penstemon (*Penstemon strictus*)
Scarlet flax (*Linum rubrum*)
Shasta daisy (*Chrysanthemum maximum*)
Tahoka daisy (*Machaeranthera tanacetifolia*)
Tickseed (*Coreopsis lanceolata*)
Toadflax (*Linaria maroccana*)
Wallflower (*Cheiranthus allionii*)
Yarrow (*Achillea millefolium*)

Wildflowers for the West

African daisy (*Dimorphotheca aurantica*)
Arroyo lupine (*Lupinus succulentus*)
Baby blue eyes (*Nemophila insignis*)
Birds eyes (*Gilia tricolor*)
Black-eyed Susan (*Rudbeckia hirta*)
Blue flax (*Linum lewisii*)
Catchfly (*Silene armeria*)
California bluebell (*Phacelia campanularia*)
California poppy (*Eschscholzia californica*)
Cornflower (*Centaurea cyanus*)
Dame's rocket (*Hesperis matronalis*)
Five spot (*Nemophila maculata*)
Evening primrose (*Oenothera lamarchiana*)
Indian blanket (*Gaillardia pulchella*)
Plains coreopsis (*Coreopsis tinctoria*)
Perennial lupine (*Lupinus perennis*)
Rocket larkspur (*Delphinium ajacis*)
Rocky Mountain penstemon (*Penstemon strictus*)
Scarlet flax (*Linum rubrum*)
Shasta daisy (*Chrysanthemum maximum*)
Tickseed (*Coreopsis lanceolata*)
Tidytips (*Layia platyglossa*)
Toadflax (*Linaria maroccana*)
Wallflower (*Cheiranthus allionii*)
Yarrow (*Achillea millefolium*)

Wildflowers for the Southwest

African daisy (*Dimorphotheca aurantica*)
Arroyo lupine (*Lupinus succulentus*)
Baby blue eyes (*Nemophila insignis*)
Black-eyed Susan (*Rudbeckia hirta*)
California bluebell (*Phacelia campanularia*)
California poppy (*Eschscholzia californica*)
Clasping coneflower (*Rudbeckia amplexicaulis*)
Five spot (*Nemophila maculata*)
Indian blanket (*Gaillardia pulchella*)
Mexican hat (*Ratibida columnaris*)
Moss verbena (*Verbena tenuisecta*)
Plains coreopsis (*Coreopsis tinctoria*)
Purple tansy (*Phacelia tanacetifolia*)
Scarlet flax (*Linum rubrum*)
Showy primrose (*Oenothera speciosa*)
Tahoka daisy (*Machaeranthera tanacetifolia*)
Tidytips (*Layia platyglossa*)
Toadflax (*Linaria maroccana*)
Yarrow (*Achillea millefolium*)

CHAPTER 5

THE LITTLE (AND NOT SO LITTLE) EXTRAS

It was the famous modern architect, Mies van der Rohe, who coined the statement, "God is in the details." As anyone who has ever tackled a large project knows, it takes true spirit and an inspired vision to see the work through to the minutest detail. Once the big construction projects—the fences, patios, decks, arbors and walkways—have been completed, and the yard has been planted the way you want it, the time finally comes to focus in on a few details— everything from such practicalities as furniture and lighting to idiosyncratic items like statues, birdhouses and ornamental containers. Some of the details may be so small you might think you're doing them only for your own enjoyment. But any sensitive soul who passes through your private outdoor retreat is sure to appreciate the totality of your creation, sensing a little of the person and the vision behind it.

FURNITURE

As outdoor living becomes second nature to more and more people, a greater selection of outdoor furniture is being made available. The options are endless: beautiful wood chairs, chaises and tables made in traditional designs; wicker furniture; metal and wrought-iron pieces good for several generations of use; canvas and wood umbrellas big enough to shield a crowd during a sudden shower; hammocks made from rope or old-fashioned canvas; and all kinds of new, "miracle" fabrics for outdoor upholstery that resist the damaging effects of the sun and extreme weather conditions.

You can adopt a casual attitude (epitomized by the European penchant for using old kitchen tables surrounded by a motley assortment of chairs) or a studied approach that dictates strict adherence to one particular style of furniture. Just remember that a garden designed for outdoor living is meant to be enjoyed with abandon. Instead of making a big design statement, feel free to err on the side of charm and informality.

Comfort and durability should be your first two concerns for outdoor furniture. Some of the most attractive chairs can be hideously uncomfortable. If you're ordering furniture from a catalog, it's not a bad idea to search out a local showroom where you can do a little comfort testing before ordering something "sight-un-sat-in." When it comes to durability, keep in mind that outdoor furniture must stand up to all types of weather, as well as considerable punishment from kids, dogs and spilled drinks, and from being hauled around from one end of the yard to the other.

Outdoor tables should be as big as they come, and definitely bigger than you think you need at the time. A big outdoor table is ideal for casual group dinners for many more people than you could or would invite over for a dinner party

Whether it's rustic bent willow chairs, or a more formal outdoor dining set, choose your outdoor furniture to blend in with its surroundings.

indoors. When spread with newspapers or a plastic tablecloth, a huge table is also a wonderful place to do art, crafts and assorted building projects—not to mention the perfect place to hold kids' birthday parties. After any messy activity, cleanup is a simple process of hosing off the table and the "floor" at the same time. Try that indoors!

The most flexible seating around any outdoor table is a pair of benches. But after sitting for a

Specialty shops and catalogs offer unusual furniture that may be just the thing for your deck or patio.

while, some people may complain about the lack of back support. If so, consider combining a few chairs with the benches. Set the chairs at the ends of the table and offer them as places of honor to any that request them. Just because you're outdoors doesn't mean that everyone can't be comfortable.

As far as siting furniture goes, two concerns are paramount: the view, and protection from the elements. Any spot in your yard where there is a particularly appealing view is the place for a couple of chairs or a bench, whether it's looking at a fountain, a valley view or a majestic oak tree backlit by the setting sun. And as wonderful as it is to be outdoors, most folks prefer to "set a spell" in a location that is protected from wind and the direct rays of the sun. If there's no protection from the sun where you want to sit, consider adding a large garden umbrella to the scene. And something as simple as a row of shrubs can be remarkably effective at dulling a prevailing wind.

If you're interested in maximum longevity and minimum upkeep for your outdoor furniture, here are a few points to remember. Any metal, be it wrought iron, steel or aluminum—can be left in its raw state, painted or powder-coated. Aluminum, of course, has the advantage of remaining rust free, even when left in its natural state, but iron and steel will rust even after one season outdoors. Traditionally, rust-inhibiting paints have been used on these materials which, as the name implies, "inhibits" but doesn't completely stop rust from forming, demanding reapplication on a regular basis. A relatively new technique, known as "powder-coating," bonds pigment (in virtually any color) electronically to the surface of the metal. Powder-coating is something of a "miracle" process, and the results are impressive—in short, no rust, and no repainting required.

Wicker has long been a favorite for outdoor furniture, but is notorious for falling prey to the damaging effects of weather rather quickly. If you're set on having wicker furniture outdoors, look for the weatherproof variety. It isn't real wicker (it's plastic-coated cellulose, wound around aluminum wire), but it's virtually impossible to tell from the real McCoy. Make no mistake about it, you'll pay a premium for this type of furniture, but it will pay off in the long term, as the best brands are guaranteed for life, even when used outdoors. This is a process that has been around since the early 1900s and, as testimony to its longevity, perfectly intact baby strollers, settees and rockers made from this synthetic wicker appear in antique stores across the country with some frequency,

White wicker furniture has long been associated with gracious outdoor living. Some types of wicker are surprisingly weather-resistant.

Many of the more modern designs are surprisingly comfortable and made of long-lasting materials.

One of most deservedly popular outdoor chairs of all time: the Adirondack chair.

although early pieces used steel wire instead of aluminum.

If you live in a climate with frequent spring and summer rainfall—and you don't want to scurry outside to remove the cushions from chairs and chaises every time it rains—by all means look into the new woven acrylic "canvas." Another "miracle" product, woven acrylic does indeed look every bit like canvas, but is virtually rot- and mildew-proof. It is available in a wide variety of colors and patterns, including all the traditional ones usually associated with cotton canvas. Choose a synthetic stuffing, and rain will quickly drain through the entire cushion and dry equally as fast once the sun comes out—a definite improvement over the old days!

There are many good-looking sets of outdoor furniture available today made from what used to be considered "exotic" woods—mahogany, teak, ipe and the like. These are extremely dense, heavy woods that stand up beautifully to the rigors of even the harshest climates. If you're interested in wooden furniture that demands next to no upkeep and that lasts for generations, this is the furniture for you. Concerns over depleted tropical forests of these valuable trees had been dealt with by responsible manufacturers who only used lumber from "farm-raised" trees—a renewable resource. If you are concerned about the state of the world's rain forests—where most of these special woods come from—favor furniture made from farm-raised lumber. Such information will be stated on the label or literature that comes with each piece of furniture.

LIGHTING

As night falls in the garden, some type of lighting will become a necessity—for safety as well as aesthetics. Just remember that a little lighting goes a long way. It is far better to be subtle than to have to shield your eyes from the glare of a misplaced or too-bright light. The goal of garden lighting is to produce a more livable outdoor area and to increase its beauty. By highlighting only the best aspects of your garden, you can create a nightscape that may be even more attractive than your daytime garden!

Low-voltage lighting systems provide just the right amount of lighting for most backyard situations. New technology has revolutionized this type of lighting, bringing it well within the installation abilities of even novice do-it-yourselfers. Modular systems and kits are so inexpensive and easy to install that outdoor lighting is finally within the reach of everyone who wants it.

Extra safety precautions need to be taken if you decide to power your outdoor lights with standard 120-volt household current. The entire system will need to be permanently installed using a direct burial grounded cable. Make sure to consult local building codes to see if a "ground-fault interrupter" is required within the circuit. On the

benefit side, the types of light fixtures available for household voltage are more suitable for large trees and where a stronger punch of illumination is desired.

When you get ready to install your system, by all means wait until after dark to experiment with placing the lights in different locations. Keep the following tips in mind as you plan and install your nightscape:

Uplighting. Aim most of your light "up." This helps keep bright lights out of the viewers' and neighbors' eyes. When you are first starting out, always keep in mind that a little light is a lot of light after dark.

Lighting a large tree. A 100-watt mercury vapor uplight is a most spectacular source of light. One light shining into a large tree produces a cool, quiet beauty, almost like moonlight. Its bluish hue enhances foliage, producing a magical effect.

Downlighting. A tree with an interesting branch structure can be accented by hanging a downlight within it. Use a commercial unit or convert an old wooden birdhouse by removing the floor and installing a small 20- or 30-watt reflector bulb within it.

Decorative garden fixtures. It is not necessary to hide all the light sources within a landscape. In fact,

Remember: A little bit of light goes a long way, especially at night. The most pleasing night-lit landscapes show considerable restraint.

some experts in the field feel that if all the light sources are hidden, viewers spend all their time trying to figure out where the light is coming from rather than enjoying the beauty of the scene. In general, decorative lighting fixtures look best located among plantings and at the edge of lawn areas. It's best not to use decorative fixtures along the sides of driveways where they will be in the way of car doors and lawn mowers. Far better to remove them from harm's way and light up the trees and shrubs immediately surrounding the driveway.

Security lighting. Existing security lights placed high under eaves will compete with softer

Low-voltage lights, artfully concealed under the lip of the stairs, provide just enough light for safety.

MOTION DETECTORS

Most large hardware and home improvement stores stock security lighting equipped with motion detectors. This impressive bit of technology allows lights to remain off until they "sense" the presence of motion, when they immediately switch on—an effective deterrent to crime. Lights equipped with motion detectors can (and should) be mounted all around the house—front, back and along the sides. Because they are completely automatic (and impressively reliable) they do not demand any attention from the owners, and they work as well when

you are at home as when you are away. Any light can be outfitted with a motion detector—from decorative front porch lights to higher wattage, utilitarian types designed to spread as much light as possible on a particular location. Most homeowners gain a considerable degree of comfort knowing such systems are in place, and research on their effectiveness indicates that comfort is well founded—these surprisingly simple systems really work.

A quick look through any outdoor living or garden catalog will reveal a variety of attractive light fixtures that blend right into the landscape.

garden lighting. If you want both types of lighting on at the same time, say for a nighttime garden party, clip blue lenses (available at large hardware stores) over the security lights to bathe the surroundings in an atmosphere of bright moonlight.

Walkways that include steps can be particularly treacherous at night: do yourself and your guests a favor and provide sufficient light for easy navigation.

Nighttime hazards. For the sake of safety, walkways, steps and edges of decks, patios and terraces should be lit at night. Fifteen-watt lamps, used in low fixtures, will be sufficient in most situations.

Attracting insects. Light attracts insects, so locate your lighting away from patios or other places where people might gather. Well-located lighting can help increase the enjoyment of your garden by keeping specific areas relatively bug free.

Dining out. If you've gone to the effort of softly lighting the rest of your landscape, you'll be surprised at how little light is needed on the dining patio. A few tabletop candles in hurricane chimneys will probably more than suffice.

TYPES OF LIGHTING

Downlighting.

Glare-free lighting.

Spotlighting.

Uplighting.

Whether it's a simple, brick-lined fire pit surrounded by benches or a gas heater permanently mounted above an elegant outdoor dining room, a little bit of warmth allows you and your guests to enjoy outdoor living both early and late in the season.

OUTDOOR HEATING

Sitting outside until long after dark can be one of the most enjoyable aspects of creating a yard for outdoor living. In areas of the country where summer evenings are cool—or to extend your outdoor living opportunities from early spring until late fall—some kind of heat will be necessary. Bear in mind that most people either run for their sweaters—or indoors altogether—once the temperature dips much below the upper 50s.

Shown here are some of the commercially available heaters for outdoor installation. Remember, you're not trying to heat the entire yard, just that one area where you and your guests are most likely to congregate and linger. That area should be physically cozy and relatively free of wind—especially at floor level.

Fire pits—both portable and permanent—are another solution to providing outdoor heat. They are highly romantic, inspiring stories that could only be told in the dark, but they also require some knowledge of fire building and, of course, extreme safety. If you've got a little of the Boy or Girl Scout left in you, however, there's simply nothing like the warmth and atmosphere of a log fire under the stars. Remember that the heat generated by an outdoor fire travels in a straight line, which is why you feel its warmth in front, but not on your back, as you face the flames. You can ameliorate this

phenomenon by enclosing the area where the fire pit is located with walls or fences that will bounce the heat back to where it's needed.

The simplest of all fire pits is a slight depression in the bare earth, ringed with large stones—primitive, but effective. If you want a fire pit directly on your brick or concrete patio, leave a space (at least 36 inches in diameter) open to the bare earth: do not attempt to build a fire directly on top of bricks or concrete, as both will be damaged from the extreme heat. Be sure to check local regulations before designing and building an outdoor fire pit as many locales have stringent requirements governing them.

Whenever you're dealing with live fire in an outdoor environment, it's a good idea to keep a hose nearby—just in case. And always keep a keen eye on children, whose fascination with fire is even more intense than an adult's. Keep in mind that this is, in fact, the outdoors, and an outdoor living space will never have all the comforts of an indoor space. Don't expect too much of outdoor heating and you won't be disappointed, since most outdoor fire sources are as much about charm as they are heat.

Masterfully designed, this outdoor fireplace says "welcome" in a big way, providing all the pleasures and comforts of indoors on an outdoor loggia.

This unique, built-in design allows for up-close enjoyment of an outdoor fireplace.

A fire pit with permanent benches creates the ambience of a campfire, right outside your back door.

Many outdoor living catalogs have started carrying portable gas patio heaters, just the thing for extending an outdoor gathering into a cool evening.

CONTAINERS & PLANTERS

Container gardeners have long known that even a small collection of various-sized containers, planted with a variety of flowering and foliage plants, can make a statement equal to a garden planted directly in the ground.

Most nurseries and garden centers stock a wide variety of containers for plants. They range from the plainest of plastic pots to terra-cotta, from concrete containers with formal designs and in bas-relief to copies of the wooden boxes in which King Louis grew his orange trees at Versailles. The simplest clay or wooden containers are fine, but a considerable amount of personality can be added to any yard with a couple of the more ornamental containers.

Choose the largest containers your budget and space can handle. They hold a greater volume of soil (which means plants won't dry out so quickly and will therefore require fewer waterings), and they add an impressive quality to the plants they contain. A pair of large containers can mark the entrance to a path, rest on either side of a wall fountain, flank the steps leading to a deck or terrace, or stand guard on

With the proper selection of plants, gardeners can create the look of a tropical jungle, completely container grown!

either side of the steps to a swimming pool. Used this way, containers, and the plants they hold, act as attractive signposts, indicating important locations in your yard. Placed right next to a door or gate, a single large container, planted with any type of flowering plant, makes for a pleasant note on which to come and go.

One issue all container gardeners have to deal with is what to do with their containers in winter.

Annuals are unbeatable when it comes to providing more or less constant color in containers.

Applying a sealant to terra-cotta pots will go a long way in helping them withstand the rigors of a harsh climate.

CARING FOR CONTAINER PLANTS

People sometimes talk about their container-grown plants as though they were pets. And like pets, they require regular care and attention—not much, mind you, but regular. In exchange, a few containers planted with flowering shrubs, annuals or perennials will offer the colorful impact of a much larger bed or border for a fraction of the work. Don't be afraid to experiment with plants not normally grown in containers. Virtually any plant (including roses) can be grown in a pot, provided it receives the proper care.

Make it easy on yourself, and fill your containers with any of the packaged, lightweight soil mixes sold in nurseries and garden centers. While you're at it, pick up some timed or slow-release fertilizer. One application at planting time should just about take care of the plant's nutrient needs for an entire growing season. Read and follow the label directions. If you notice the plants waning late in the season (symptoms include yellowing leaves and fewer flowers), make a second application of fertilizer.

In addition to using a good soil mix and making sure there are enough nutrients available, remember to water your container-grown plants on a regular basis. During hot, dry weather, they will need a good soaking every day. And if you're leaving home for even one summer weekend, have someone water the container plants for you.

In areas of the country with mild winters, terra-cotta (red clay) pots can be left outdoors year-round without any fear of damage. Because terra-cotta is porous, the walls of the pots will always contain some amount of water. Where winters are severe, periods of alternate freezing and thawing will eventually take their toll, resulting in cracked and crumbling pots. If they are not too heavy, you can avoid this problem by moving the pots into your garage or basement for the winter. If you can't move them, paint the pots both inside and out with a liberal coating of water sealant. By doing so, you'll extend the life of the pots considerably.

If the hassle of moving terra-cotta pots back and forth is just too much, take a look at the new generation of fiberglass and plastic planters; they've come a long way in terms of both longevity and good looks. New manufacturing techniques and ways to apply finishes have resulted in very sturdy containers, available in any number of shapes and sizes (including very large ones), and a variety of finishes, ranging from ones that look like concrete to others that resemble weathered copper or terra-cotta. Even up close, these containers are virtually impossible to tell from the real thing: they're lightweight and represent an excellent value for the money. Best of all, they can be left outdoors through the winter, in even the most severe of climates.

If weight is not a consideration, concrete containers stand up well to even the most extreme cold, without the flaking or cracking associated with terra-cotta. If the gray color of concrete is not to your liking, it can be stained any color you wish. Mix some artist's oil color (available in tubes at art supply stores) with a little paint thinner until it is runny. Soak an old rag in the pigment and rub and daub it onto the concrete for a permanent stain. This is a messy job, so be sure to have plenty of newspapers around to soak up any spilled or splotched paint.

CONTAINER CANDIDATES

When it comes time to plant in your containers, the best candidates are plants that are relatively tidy and compact. Plants that shed leaves or drop fruit, along with those that quickly grow out-of-bounds, are often more trouble than they are worth. The following two lists are divided between upright plants and trailing plants; the best container plantings usually combine some of each.

Upright Growers

Ageratum (annual)
Bamboo (shrub)
Caladium (perennial)
Chrysanthemum (perennial)
Coleus (annual)
Coreopsis (perennial)
Cosmos (annual)
Geranium (upright form, perennial)
Hydrangea (shrub)
Impatiens (annual)
Lily of the Nile (tender perennial)
Marigold (annual)
New Zealand flax (perennial)
Nicotiana (annual)
Pansy (annual)
Penstemon (perennial)
Primrose (perennial)
Roses, especially floribunda types (shrub)
Rudbeckia (perennial)
Salvia (annual)
Zinnia (annual)

Trailing Plants

Alyssum (annual)
Black-eyed Susan vine (annual)
Browallia (annual)
English Ivy (perennial)
Ivy geranium (perennial)
Lobelia (annual)
Nasturtium (annual)
Petunia (annual)
Sanvitalia (annual)
Verbena (annual)
Vinca (annual and perennial)

Well-chosen and positioned container plants can go a long way in softening the effect of large patios and decks.

A container of hydrangea.

A collection of cacti and succulents.

It's hard to beat container-grown flowering plants for their ability to instantly dress up any space.

White trailing alyssum.

Big-flowered hydrangea.

ORNAMENTAL ACCESSORIES

Ornamental accessories for your outdoor living room include everything from statuary, wall plaques, sundials, birdbaths, antique wheelbarrows, flags, tile work and plastic trolls to gazing balls—and much, much more.

Used "correctly," ornamental accessories direct the viewer's eye to it, which is why the English call such accessories "eye-catchers." Often they are just the thing—whether that "thing" is a statue of Venus, or a Victorian birdhouse—that sparks a garden scene into life, transforming it from dull to memorable. When you're looking for a garden accent, it pays to experiment: where a large, dark Louis XV urn does nothing, a sundial on a light-colored column may be just what's needed. Trust your own eye when experimenting with accessories; you'll instinctively know when something is "just right."

Virtually every home and garden designer in the world would probably say that it's possible to have too much of a good thing, telling anyone who might ask: "By all means, limit yourself to one major, eye-catching piece, and leave the rest on the showroom floor." Tasteful advice, to be sure, but some of the most charming yards ever created sport one bit of ornament after another—here a concrete cherub peering out from the ferns, there a collection of antique water cans and, behind that, a weatherbeaten garden troll, contentedly puffing on his pipe. Too much, by far, for most people, but when it's an accurate reflection of what pleases the owner, it's just right, and so be it.

Tradition, rather than taste, offers a few reliable guidelines for the unsure: important ornaments, such as an imposing piece of statuary or a huge Chinese urn, need to be highlighted. Place them at the end of a line of sight—at the far end of a lawn, at the

A delightful arched doorway tucked into a masonry wall, and surrounded by vining plants.

termination of a walkway or at the end of a tunnel of trees.

More modest ornaments, such as birdbaths and sundials, are good for giving geometrically shaped beds a focal point. They should be placed directly in the center of the bed.

These suggestions have been followed since people first began making gardens, and they continue to produce desirable results. And if you use a birdbath, hopefully it will be in a place where you can enjoy it, because they are much more than merely ornamental. If you keep birdbaths full of fresh water on a regular basis, birds really will visit frequently; it would be a shame to miss all that action if the birdbath were located in some far-off corner of the yard.

Although they don't require much in the way of maintenance, birdbaths should be kept free of algae and slime with regular brushing from a stiff brush (or broom) and plenty of water. Refrain from using any disinfectant, such as

Outdoor ornamental accessories run the gamut from paintings (yes, you can hang paintings outdoors if you want to!) to gazing balls like this.

chlorine, which, in too high of a concentration can be harmful to birds and other visitors to your birdbath. Always keep your birdbath filled with plenty of clean water—once they know where it is, your feathered friends will quickly come to depend on it for a supply of water.

If you have functioning birdhouses in your garden—ones meant to be used as nesting sites—they should be completely cleaned and disinfected once a year, after the nest has been abandoned by the parents and youngsters. Remove all the nesting material, clean the interior with a stiff brush and plenty of water, and then disinfect the walls with a weak solution of chlorine bleach and water (one-half cup of chlorine bleach to a gallon of water). Allow the nesting box or birdhouse to air out and completely dry before placing it back in the yard.

A word of warning: If you have any old or valuable pieces of garden statuary in public view, make sure that they are very securely anchored. A recent surge of interest in "antique" garden ornaments has led to increased value and, unfortunately, theft.

A birdbath is functional—for the birds—but it can also be pretty to look at even when feathered visitors aren't about.

A collection of ornamental birdhouses dresses up a corner of the garden.

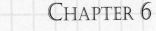

CHAPTER 6

OUTDOOR EATING & ENTERTAINING

I n an outdoor setting, it's only natural that life's tempo slows down a bit. Your family or guests may sit back and notice the sound of the birds, the dance of the shadows across the table, or the colors of the setting sun. Because the environment is so pleasant, people don't seem to rush through their meal—whether it's a celebratory feast or just a weeknight dinner—the way they sometimes might indoors. They're willing to sit a little longer around the table, chatting or simply enjoying the surroundings. And if you're a cook looking for compliments (and what cook isn't?), fresh air sharpens people's appetites, so anything you prepare is going to taste that much better.

FOR THE OUTDOOR CHEF

What does the outdoor cook need? Other than the grill itself—examples of which can be seen on these pages—by all means, set up an attractive place to put it (if it's attractive enough, maybe you'll attract the cook out there a little more often). Nothing complements an outdoor dining room more than food that's been cooked over the coals!

As to the needs of the outdoor chef, here's a short list of what's important: (1) a pleasant view, (2) a stool, (3) some kind of light, (4) a small table and (5) some protection from rain (if necessary).

The first requirement, a pleasant view, will help immeasurably in producing a beneficial frame of mind. Don't place your grill where the only thing you see is the

neighbor's untidy yard, a couple of air-conditioning units in the side yard, or a storage shed. Walk around a bit before rolling your grill into position.

Once you find the perfect spot, outfit it with something to sit on, such as a wooden stool or bench, and a small, sturdy table for landing platters full of food. Set up some kind of a light, even if it's a large flashlight, so you can see what the food looks like when it's dark outside.

Selecting a Grill

Although there are many variations, there are basically only two choices when it comes to grill design: covered and uncovered. And there are strong feelings regarding these two choices.

People who don't like covered grills complain about the fact that you can't adjust the cooking grill (or the bed of coals) up or down to control the temperature. Others resent the fact that to be used properly—the way they were designed to be used—covered grills should be used with the cover on. On the other hand, people who endorse covered grills say that once

Recent years have seen an explosion of products—everything from stoves to refrigerators and icemakers—especially designed for outdoor use. These outdoor kitchens rival any indoor one, and come with a price tag to match.

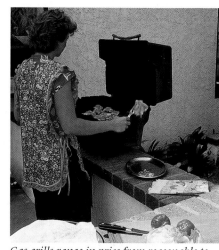

Gas grills range in price from reasonable to downright expensive. That said, a moderately-priced unit will more than suffice for most outdoor cooks.

you get used to cooking on them, and to their versatility in terms of smoking and cooking large roasts and whole turkeys and chickens, it's hard to go back to the limitations of an open grill.

If you've done much grilling, you know that an open grill works great for hamburgers, hot dogs, steaks or fish—in short, anything that doesn't demand much time on the grill. But any cut of meat that needs to be roasted as much as it does grilled, such as a leg of lamb, pork tenderloin, or beef brisket, is almost impossible to cook successfully on an open grill. Given that you can grill hamburgers, hot dogs, steaks and fish on a covered grill, it just may be that they are the superior grill for all-around use.

Gas or Charcoal?

No doubt about it, gas grills are increasing in popularity every year. Their ease of use and no-muss, no-fuss starting seem to be the big attraction, and it's hard to argue with these facts. But a true-blue

charcoal griller will be slow to give up his or her charcoal-powered grill, simply because they are as much in love with the whole process of starting the fire, waiting for the coals to get just right and the smoky aroma, as they are with the results that come from the grill. In the end, choosing between a gas grill and a charcoal one is an entirely

With their cleanliness and ease of operation, there's a lot to be said for the convenience of gas grills.

subjective decision. If you do, however, decide on a gas grill, here are a few things to keep in mind:

One—you don't always get what you pay for. The price in gas grills ranges from about $200 to over $3,000. You can get a good grill for about $600. Price, however, is not the only thing to keep in mind when buying a grill. Consider how the grill will be used: do you intend to entertain on a large scale, or for one or two of you? The answer to that question determines the size of the grilling surface you'll need and, perhaps less importantly, the size of the working areas (the "landing pads") on both sides of the grill. Some grills are fine for a steak or a couple of burgers, but are not suitable for racks of ribs or a turkey.

Another feature you'll want as a serious griller is a temperature gauge that reads in degrees—not just high, medium and low. And if you've ever run out of propane on a Sunday night, right in the middle of preparing a grilled feast,

Everybody's Favorite Flank Steak

In their favor, flank steaks are one of the tastiest (and leanest) cuts of beef, they cook up in a hurry and, given their large surface area, they take well to marinades. Without the tenderizing effect of a marinade, however, flank steaks can be tough, so plan on marinating these steaks for at least an hour before grilling.

Flank steak, cut into thin slices at about a 45-degree angle, are excellent for making into delicious steak sandwiches. Here's how:

Cut a baguette, or similar long loaf of coarse bread, down the middle, lengthwise. Brush sparingly with softened butter, margarine or olive oil. Grill the bread until just toasted. Spread both sides of the bread with a mixture of equal parts mayonnaise and Dijon mustard, or equal parts mayonnaise and grated horseradish. Top with slices of flank steak (recipe at right), thin rounds of red onion, tomato and lettuce. Put top slice of bread in place and cut the sandwich into 4-inch-long pieces. Good eating!

FLANK STEAK

1 flank steak

For the marinade:
1/4 cup vegetable or olive oil
1/4 cup soy sauce
1/2 cup dry sherry
2 cloves garlic, minced
1 small onion, minced
1 1/2 teaspoons ground dry ginger
1 to 2 teaspoons freshly ground pepper

1) In a marinating dish, mix together all the marinade ingredients. Place flank steak in the marinade, turning several times to coat both sides. Cover with plastic wrap and marinate at least 1 hour before grilling. Turn flank steak once or twice while marinating.

2) Preheat the grill for 10 to 15 minutes. When ready to grill, turn one of the burners off and the others to medium.

3) Sear the flank steak quickly (approximately 1 to 2 minutes per side) directly over one of the burners that is on. After searing, move the steak over the burner that is off for a total of 18 to 20 minutes, turning once, halfway through the cooking time. This will produce a medium steak. Adjust cooking time slightly up or down to produce a more well done or rarer steak.

4) After grilling, place steak on a cutting board and allow to rest for 5 minutes. Using a sharp carving knife held at a 45-degree angle, cut flank steak into thin slices. Serve with juices accumulated on the cutting board. Can be served hot off the grill or at room temperature. Serves 4, generously.

a built-in gas gauge on the supply tanks is something that could hardly be considered an "extra."

With good gas grills, the entire grilling surface produces consistent, even heat with no hot or cool spots. Just as important, grease should be funneled away to a drip pan, removing the possibility of flare-ups or grease fires—or just as bad, of burned food.

Over time, grills outfitted with lava rocks seem to absorb the grease and have the nasty habit of flaring up on their own, and even some of the most expensive lava-rock grills have inconsistent heat from one side of the grill to the other. Gas grills with V-shaped channels—in place of lava rocks—seem to be the most efficient in producing even heat, reducing flare-ups and keeping the grease directed to the drip pan.

Some high-end gas grills tout their ability to produce very high temperatures. While such grills may seem desirable at first, they also have a tendency to burn food rapidly, long before the interior of your food has cooked adequately. A grill that can reach 550°F produces more than adequate heat to properly sear whatever type of food you are cooking.

Smokers

Smoking units for the home chef are commonplace these days. In their favor, these smokers probably offer the closest reproduction of the famous barbecue joints of the Midwest, Southeast and Southwest—a way to cook meats over a low, smoky fire for long periods of time ("low-and-slow" as the barbecue pitmasters say).

You can turn out some fabulous food using these cookers—especially large cuts of beef, venison and other wild game, pork and the like—but don't expect them to perform at their best as a standard charcoal grill, because that's not what they were designed for. If you go in for smoking foods in a big way, the ideal would be to have a standard charcoal or gas grill and a smoker.

Wood-Fired Ovens

Wood-fired ovens were a common accessory in rural Italian homes until just after World War II. The postwar years brought with them the desire for things modern, and the wood-fired oven all but became a thing of the past. There were those, however, who remembered the joys of an outdoor oven, and the unforgettable aromas and flavors these ovens produced. Luckily, enough craftspeople remembered how to construct these ovens, and recent years have seen a resurgence of interest in and availability of home wood-fired ovens.

Outdoor cooking is as much theater as it is anything else. Relax, take your time, gather a hungry audience and put on a delicious show.

High-profile American chefs, such as Alice Waters and Wolfgang Puck, eager to capture the rustic flavors of European country cooking, had wood-fired ovens installed in their restaurants. The appeal of these ovens is so great, that unlike other kitchen "appliances," these wood-fired ovens were placed in full view of the dining-room patrons. There is something undeniably satisfying about using one of these ovens that speaks directly to the joys of cooking—not the least of which is the way the food tastes after it's done. You can double that satisfaction if the wood-fired oven is outdoors, right in your own backyard.

Although the wood-fired oven practically disappeared from Europe, along with the knowledge of how to construct one, enough craftspeople remembered that a "new" industry was born. An American by the name of Renato Riccio (a native of Tuscany) began importing the wood-fired ovens from Italy. The demand finally became so great that Riccio decided to manufacture the ovens in America. His company, Renato Specialty Products, Inc., is to this day the only domestic manufacturer of wood-fired ovens—"an old-world experience built with modern-day technology," as Riccio says.

If you are at all titillated by the idea of owning a wood-fired oven (think of the bread you could bake!), call or write Renato Specialty Products at: (214) 349-5296, 11350 Pagemill, Dallas, TX 75243. Ask them to send you the brochure on "la magia del fuoco" (the magic of a fire). But be prepared to be tempted by the magic!

The Outdoor Cupboard

If it makes you nervous to use your indoor plates, dishes and glassware outdoors, leave them where they are. It's far better to invest in a set of dishes and glasses made of plastic, tin or some other nonbreakable material, and relax when you're eating outdoors.

Conveniently tucked under an outdoor counter, this small refrigerator receives plenty of use during the summer season.

Another practical alternative to purchasing a special outdoor set of dishes is to set aside all the chipped or cracked pieces of crockery and designate them as your special outdoor set of china. Keep all your outdoor supplies corralled in one location so you, or whoever might be helping you set the table, can easily identify which set is which.

ESSENTIAL ACCESSORIES FOR THE OUTDOOR CHEF

The list of accessories that are truly necessary for the outdoor cook is mercifully short. Just remember to buy the best quality available and always keep them in the same place so you remember where to find them from one grilling occasion to the next.

Spring-loaded tongs:

Tongs.

Professional grill cooks do a lot of their work with spring-loaded, stainless-steel tongs. With a little practice, you will find you can turn almost any cut of meat, as well as brochettes of seafood, whole fish, small game birds—just about anything except for fish fillets—with these tongs. Because they are spring-loaded, they are much easier to handle than the scissor-action tongs found in most home kitchens.

Offset spatula:

Next to tongs, the other indispensable tool of professional grill cook is a long-bladed offset spatula. These come in a range of sizes, but the most useful size has a blade 7$\frac{1}{2}$ by 3 inches, large enough to lift a whole delicate fish fillet. Spatulas made for home use are rarely more than 4 or 5 inches long, big enough for a hamburger, but not for a whole fish fillet. The home models also tend to be rather flimsy. With a proper professional spatula, you can use the length and stiffness of the blade to simultaneously scrape and lift food off the grill.

Skewers:

Skewers.

A good skewer must not only hold small pieces of food together, it must also keep them from rotating on the skewer each time the skewer is turned. For this reason, look for metal skewers that have a flattened oval shape instead of round.

Basting brush:

A good-sized brush is useful for oiling the grill before heating, for brushing a little oil on fish or vegetables before cooking, and for applying marinades or other flavorings to food already on the grill. A 2- or 3-inch paintbrush type with natural bristles is the most useful size. Long-handled brushes are available if you prefer to work a greater distance from the fire.

Thermometers:

There are several ways to tell when specific foods are done, but none is as precise and objective as a meat thermometer. The instant-read thermometer is probably the easiest to use. It is similar to a standard meat thermometer, but it registers the internal temperature of food within a couple of seconds. Standard meat thermometers are just as useful as instant-read thermometers, but they must be left in the food for several minutes to register the correct temperature.

Thermometer.

Outdoor Food

Just as with dishes, the test for anything to do with food outdoors is that if it makes you nervous, leave it inside. The first rule in outdoor cooking is "the simpler, the better."

Outdoor food can be as satisfying as any in the world, but it should not be fussed over. Find the freshest, best ingredients and let their natural flavors speak for themselves. Herbs—perhaps fresh from your own garden—are a natural accompaniment to outdoor foods, for any course, from soup to dessert.

The best trick for enjoying outdoor meals, especially when they are being served to a group, is to start preparing the food early and serve everything either cold or at room temperature. Hot dogs and hamburgers, as easy as they are to prepare, must be prepared at the last minute and served hot off the grill—which is usually when appetites are at their maximum and patience at a minimum. On the other hand, grilled chicken, a thick steak cut into thin strips, or any skewered meat-and-vegetable combination can be cooked well ahead of mealtime and served whenever everyone's ready to eat. Look at it this way: If it's warm enough to eat outdoors, it's warm enough for cool food.

There are those who say that some food actually tastes better at room temperature than it does hot. If, however, the interval between cooking the food and serving it is more than an hour, store the cooked food in the refrigerator until about 30 minutes prior to the meal. The best part about pre-preparing an outdoor meal is how relaxed you'll be by the time the guests arrive and the only thing left to do is to enjoy your own party!

Beautifully constructed of clear redwood lumber, this outdoor kitchen utilizes a very simple design.

Pandora's Turkey

Do you want to have the best turkey you've ever eaten this Thanksgiving (or any other day, for that matter)? Do you want to sleep in on Thanksgiving morning, instead of getting up at 6 a.m. to put the turkey in the oven? All you really need to accomplish this seemingly magical feat is a covered kettle grill, a 10-pound bag of charcoal and the turkey. True, this procedure requires hanging out in the backyard when most folks are thinking of warming their toes by the fire, but the results are so spectacular that they are well worth putting on an extra sweater and warm socks. (Note: If Thanksgiving Day dawns really cold and blustery, roll the grill to some protected spot close to the house, like on the back porch; that's why the grill has wheels on it.)

Before you get started, here are a few tips:

• Look for a bird that is as squat as possible; a high breastbone will prevent the lid of the grill from closing completely. Turkeys in the 18- to 22-pound range seem to fit best. If you want a larger bird, it's not a bad idea to do a test before you unwrap the bird. Simply place the turkey on the grill (not lit, of course), and make sure the lid completely closes (for birds larger than 22 pounds, ignite an extra pound of charcoal and add an additional 30 minutes to the cooking time).

• Roast the turkey with an aromatic stuffing, one that is not meant for eating, as outlined below. If you choose this route and plan on making stock from the turkey carcass afterward, hang onto the aromatic stuffing; it will improve the taste of the stock.

• There will be plenty of juices in the roasting pan. These can be divided between the gravy pot and for moistening the oven-cooked stuffing. So far there haven't been any complaints in the stuffing department. In fact, no one has ever detected that it wasn't cooked inside the bird.

PANDORA'S TURKEY

Equipment and ingredients needed:
A covered, kettle-type grill
5 pounds charcoal briquettes
18- to 22-pound turkey (larger, if it will fit on your grill, covered)
2 yellow onions
5 ribs celery
2 tablespoons poultry seasoning or dried sage
1/2 cup vegetable oil or melted butter (for rubbing on the outside of the turkey)
Salt, or seasoned salt if you prefer
Pepper
A few metal or bamboo skewers (or needle and cotton thread for trussing)

• Turkeys cooked in covered kettle grills don't need basting. In fact, if you take the lid off to baste the bird (or even just to peek), you'll blow the whole process. The rapid influx of air causes the coals to heat up quickly, resulting in an uneven cooking temperature and shortening the life of the coals. So leave the lid on the grill until the fire goes out. You know what happened to Pandora …

1) Start with a clean grill, free of old coals and ash. Ignite approximately 5 pounds of briquettes. Five pounds may seem like a lot, but this is a special procedure. If you have difficulty determining 5 pounds, simply buy a 10-pound bag of charcoal and use half.

2) While you're waiting for the coals to catch, prepare the turkey for cooking. Remove the neck and giblets from inside the bird; reserve for making gravy, if desired. Wash the bird thoroughly with cold water. (Don't use soap, like one of my mother's very tidy friends once did!) Pat dry with a towel, absorbing as much moisture, inside and out, as possible. Place the turkey in one of those disposable, heavy-duty aluminum roasting pans, available at supermarkets and variety stores.

3) Coarsely chop the onions and celery. Put in a large bowl and mix with 1/2 cup melted butter and 1 to 2 tablespoons of poultry seasoning or sage. Place a handful of this aromatic mixture inside the neck cavity. Pull the skin over the cavity and thread it closed, using a small metal or bamboo skewer. Put the rest of the mixture in the body cavity and fasten closed with another skewer. Secure the legs to the tail using the metal fastener found on most turkeys, or abandon the skewers and the metal fasteners altogether in favor of trussing the bird (provided that someone, somewhere taught you how to perform this procedure).

4) Rub the entire surface of the turkey with about 1/2 cup of melted butter or vegetable oil. Place the turkey, breast side up, in the roasting pan and sprinkle liberally with salt and pepper. I prefer finely ground white pepper because it adheres to the surface better than the coarser black pepper. Feel free to used seasoned salt, if desired.

5) Check the fire. The coals are just right when they are completely covered with fine gray ash. Once at that stage (usually in 20 to 25 minutes), push them to either side of the fire grate in equal quantities, leaving the center free of

briquettes. Put the cooking grill in place. Position the roasting pan and turkey in the middle of the grill and put the lid on. Leave both the top and bottom vents completely open.

6) Within minutes you will start to hear some action in the roasting pan and smell that delightful aroma. The turkey will be done when the coals have burned out, usually around 2 1/2 hours. You can tell the coals have burned out when the turkey no longer makes any cooking noises inside the grill and smoke has stopped coming out of the vents.

7) Remove the lid—finally— and voilà! A beautifully roasted, mahogany-brown, crisp-on-the-outside, moist-on-the-inside turkey. Carefully move the bird from the roasting pan to the carving board, and let it rest for 15 to 20 minutes before carving. This allows the juices to return to the interior of the meat and makes the turkey much easier to carve. Add any juices that accumulate on the carving board to your gravy, or use for moistening the stuffing.

MARINADES

What we call a marinade today has its roots in the distant past, long before modern refrigeration. For centuries, brine solutions and pickling techniques were used as preservatives to increase the storage life of fresh meats. Regionally favored herb and spice blends were often added to these preserving solutions to offset their harsh flavor. Gradually, food storage methods improved, but by then, whole populations had become accustomed to particular spice and herb mixtures combined with certain foods.

Today, these flavors are all but synonymous with regional cuisines from around the world and have made their way into a variety of marinades and sauces. Thus we have curry-yogurt marinades and sauces from India, soy-ginger-garlic-pepper mixtures from the Orient and chili blends from Spain and Mexico. And the list goes on.

While it is true that cooking within a particular ethnic or cultural style requires certain ingredients, the making of a marinade within any specific tradition is still open to customizing.

Unlike baking, an exact science demanding careful measurement and attention to detail, marinades the world over are fast and loose. As long as you include a liquid, an oil and some flavoring, you have the basis for a marinade. In the beginning, you may find yourself using every spice and herb in the rack, just because you can. Over time, you'll find your favorites and, most likely, your marinades will become quite simple.

All it takes to make a marinade is to combine the ingredients in a bowl and mix them thoroughly. The best containers in which to marinate foods are made of noncorrosive materials such as glass, plastic or glazed earthenware. Other materials may contribute "off" flavors to the marinade and, ultimately, the food. Use a container that's big and deep enough so the food can be positioned in a single layer and easily turned to coat both sides. Foods that are marinated for longer than 2 hours (at room temperature) should be refrigerated. In this case, you will need a container with a cover. Lacking an acceptable container, virtually all marinating can be done in tightly sealed, heavy-duty plastic bags.

How long it takes depends on how strongly you want the food flavored, the strength of the marinade and the type of food being marinated.

Obviously, for subtle flavor enhancement, marinate for short time periods, especially if the marinade is strong.

Fish should rarely be marinated for more than 30 to 45 minutes, especially if the marinade contains an acid component such as wine, citrus juice or vinegar. This also holds true with boned, skinless chicken breasts. Marinating too long will cause the fibers of the meat to break down, producing an unappealing, mushy texture. Generally speaking, high-quality foods have excellent flavors of their own that shouldn't be masked by over marinating.

Don't be fooled by how a marinade tastes straight. A strong marinade may be very unpleasant when sipped from a spoon but excellent when used on meat and cooked over coals. This is often the case with soy marinades.

Some marinades take a long time to absorb the flavor of herbs and spices, especially if you use dried herbs. For recipes that call for a short marinating period, make the marinade several hours in advance so it can develop its full flavor before the food is added.

PORK TENDERLOIN WITH DIJON MUSTARD GLAZE

This recipe is the essence of simplicity: the pork loins are coated with a Dijon mustard mixture, allowed to sit for a bit and then grilled. It's a great flavor combination and there's virtually no waste. 2 pork tenderloins, 3/4 to 1 pound apiece.

For the marinade:
1/2 cup Dijon mustard
3 tablespoons olive oil
3 cloves garlic, pressed
1/4 teaspoon freshly ground pepper

1) Combine all the ingredients for the marinade and mix well. Place the pork tenderloins in a shallow container and cover with the mustard marinade, coating them thoroughly. Allow to marinate, in the refrigerator, for 30 to 60 minutes. Remove from the refrigerator approximately 15 minutes prior to grilling.

2) Preheat the grill for 10 to 15 minutes, with all burners on high.

3) Once the grill has been preheated, turn one of the burners off and the others to

medium.
Place the tenderloins over the burner which has been turned off. Cook with the lid closed for 25 to 35 minutes, turning once or twice during the cooking process.

4) When the tenderloins are cooked, remove from the grill and slice on the thin side. Serves 6 to 8.

Marinades can transform even inexpensive cuts of meat and poultry into delicious fare for an outdoor meal.

TEMPERATURE CHART FOR MEAT AND POULTRY

Food	Rare	Medium	Well Done
Beef	140°F	160°F	170-180°F
Lamb	140°F	160°F	170°F
Pork*	160°F	170°F	
Poultry		All domestic poultry should be cooked to 185°F	

* The U.S.D.A. now considers 137°F as the temperature
at which the parasites that cause trichinosis are destroyed.

CHAPTER 7

HOT TUBS & SPAS

For thousands of years, many cultures—from ancient Greece and Rome to the Near East and Japan—have appreciated the benefits of a good, hot soak. They might not have known exactly why the hot water made them feel good, but it was enough that it did. Both public and private hot water soaking lasted as a popular leisure time activity for countless generations.

Today, according to some medical authorities, a good soak in a spa or hot tub is a form of preventive medicine—a means of avoiding illness. Spas and hot tubs offer a drug-free way of reducing stress, while offering relaxation, encouraging socialization and reducing anxiety. Skin-temperature measurements help illustrate the relaxing qualities of hot water. A skin temperature of 86°F to 88°F signals stress. A skin temperature of 93°F to 94°F indicates deep relaxation. A hot soak can reduce tension, which is a contributor to high blood pressure, heart disease, ulcers and other stress-related health problems.

WHERE TO PUT THEM

Strategically placed at the far corner of a deck, this acrylic spa takes full advantage of the surrounding views.

Most spas and hot tubs can be installed, inspected and ready to use within a few days. You can put them indoors or out, below ground, partially below ground or completely above ground. You'll find spas and hot tubs on patios, decks and roofs, or in family rooms, basements and greenhouses—just about anywhere that's conducive to a good, relaxing soak.

Where you decide to put your hot tub or spa involves a number of

decisions. Do you want the spa or tub indoors or out? If it is outdoors, remember that soaking in a spa or tub is essentially an intimate experience. Most people desire a location with a certain degree of privacy.

Every yard will offer several potential sites; get to know them by walking around your entire yard. Think how it would feel to be in a spa or tub in different locations. If your spa is going to be sunk into the ground, get down on your hands

and knees to see what the view and feeling are like from that vantage point. As you walk around your yard, stray off the beaten path to see what the view is like from seldom-used areas. Compare potential views beyond your property, because it's a real bonus to have a pleasant view when you're sitting in a spa or tub.

Look for sites sheltered from the wind as much as possible. Wind is not only uncomfortable for soakers, but it also blows leaves and other debris into the spa or tub. Cool winds blowing across the water's surface will rob heat from the spa or tub, which means the heater must work overtime to keep the water at the desired temperature. Wind-free areas may be protected by mature shrubs or trees, or by nearby structures, such as buildings or fences.

To find these sites, attach strips of lightweight cloth or ribbons to 3-foot-tall stakes and place them around the yard on a typically breezy day. The amount of fluttering and flying they produce will be a good indicator of wind direction and force at various sites.

How far from the house should you place your unit? A closer location may ensure more use. This is especially true if you plan to use it primarily for a quick soak before retiring. If children are going to use the spa or tub, by all means place it where it will be close to and in full view of the house.

If you live on a sloping or contoured lot, avoid locating in-ground spas or tubs in natural drainage areas or runoff slopes. You'll want irrigation and rainwater to drain away from the tub or spa, not into it.

This redwood hot tub has been skillfully integrated into the surrounding wooden deck.

Intricately laid flagstones not only incorporate this spa into the landscape, but create a convenient place for bathers to sit.

Raising a spa above the deck level not only makes getting in and out easier, but also creates a sitting area around its perimeter.

CHOOSING A SPA OR TUB

Spas and hot tubs are used for the same purposes: hydrotherapy and relaxation. But there are significant differences between spas and tubs—even between kinds of spas. It will pay to consider these differences before you decide which type to install.

Spas. The most popular spas are molded fiberglass units with an interior-finish, nonporous surface of acrylic or gelcoat. This combination gives strong, watertight, one-piece construction. In this respect, they're like large bathtubs or small swimming pools. Most fiberglass spas are located outdoors but can be put indoors as well. These lightweight shells are commonly sunk below ground, but with proper support you can install them partially or completely above ground level.

Unfortunately, a misconception about spa types has persisted for a number of years. People frequently ask: "Which is better, fiberglass or acrylic?" In truth, the acrylic spa is a fiberglass shell with a top surface of solid, molded acrylic. What many refer to as a fiberglass spa is one with a gelcoat surface.

Most pool maintenance companies will tell you fiberglass spas—acrylic or gelcoat—are easier to maintain than wooden tubs or concrete or Gunite spas. Their non-porous surface makes thorough cleaning a simple process, and leakage is not a concern.

Concrete Spas. With most concrete spas, concrete is pneumatically applied by a machine over a network of tied steel reinforcing bars. Gunite or Shotcrete is an almost-dry mixture of cement and sand, shot from a nozzle at high pressure. Poured concrete spas are less common, requiring the building of wooden forms.

Concrete spas are often attached to swimming pools. The spa's interior surface usually has a smooth plaster finish and a band of ceramic tile rimming the spa at the waterline to make cleaning easier. In fact, some concrete spas are completely covered with ceramic tile, an expensive but attractive alternative.

There are several advantages to Gunite or Shotcrete spas. They can be created in almost any custom shape, often to complement the design of an adjoining pool. There are, however, disadvantages: both materials require skilled workmanship and an experienced builder. Gunite and Shotcrete must

Deck boards radiating out from this spa make for an interesting design.

be sprayed evenly to ensure uniform wall thickness of the spa shell. And the total cost of a custom concrete spa is usually considerably more than that of other types of spas and tubs.

Portable Spas. These spas consist of a molded fiberglass spa, heater, pump, filter, hydrojets or bubbler or both, and a skirt that hides the working parts of the spas. All that's required to install most portable spas is an acceptable location (most importantly, one that can support the weight of the filled spa), an electrical outlet and a nearby source of water.

Spas Attached to Swimming Pools. Many people find a cool dip in the swimming pool a refreshing way to end a hot soak in the spa. If the spa is attached to a pool, both spa and pool can use the same filtration and heating system. Depending on personal preference and use requirements, a separate filtration system may be required.

Hot Tubs. The original hot tubs were recycled water or wine barrels. Not surprisingly, the term hot tub always refers to a large, watertight, wooden tub.

Hot tub builders still employ old-world coopering, or barrel-making techniques, in tub construction. The tub sides consist of bevel-cut, vertical staves, grooved to fit snugly around the tub bottom. Hoops or flat bands lock the staves together. When the tub is filled with water, the wood expands, making all the joints watertight. Tubs can be of redwood, teak, mahogany, cedar, cypress, oak or other suitable wood resistant to decay and the chemicals used to keep the water clean.

A small amount of leakage, called weeping, sometimes occurs with wooden tubs. Keeping the water at its optimum level prevents staves from contracting and keeps leakage to a minimum. Tub sizes vary dramatically—from 2 1/2 feet to 5 feet deep and from 3 1/2 feet to more than 12 feet in diameter. Popular family-sized tubs are 5 to 6 feet in diameter, and 4 feet deep.

A simple gazebo-like structure, combined with lattice panels, helps provide privacy for this spa.

All the comforts of home while taking a good, hot soak.

Purists love the natural materials of wooden hot tubs.

TUB & SPA CONSIDERATIONS

Proponents of hot tubs like the neutral quality of wood. They feel it blends in well with an outdoor setting. Concrete spas can have almost any look—from that of a classic Roman bath to a natural-looking hot spring. Acrylic spas may be less natural-looking, but the choice of designs, shapes, sizes and colors is greater. This versatility, along with the fact that they are easier to clean than either wooden or concrete spas, makes acrylic spas the most popular choice of all.

On the plus side for tubs: You can generally buy hot tubs in smaller sizes to fit tight spaces. On the down side: in tubs, bathers must sit upright, whereas in spas, the molded seats offer a number of relaxed, lounging positions.

Chemical maintenance and heating costs are roughly the same for spas and hot tubs, but note that there are differences when it comes to portability. Many hot tubs are placed on a deck or patio—not sunk into the ground—making them portable, in a sense. If you decide to move a hot tub, it can be dismantled, but it's not an easy job. Any in-ground spa is a permanent improvement to your property and cannot be moved.

Heat loss is also a consideration: wood is a better insulator than molded fiberglass or concrete. Studies have shown that water in an above-ground redwood hot tub with an insulating cover drops only about 10°F in 24 hours, at an ambient temperature of approximately 55°F. An uninsulated, partially above ground fiberglass spa can lose more than twice that amount of heat.

Large, smooth river stones give this spa a natural look.

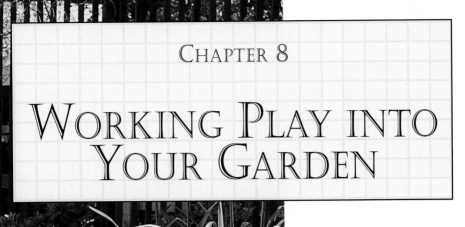

CHAPTER 8

WORKING PLAY INTO YOUR GARDEN

One of the best—and most overlooked—benefits to a yard set up for outdoor living is the opportunities it provides for having fun and playing games. If you have children in your household, or regularly play host to them in your yard, the conditions found in almost any backyard are fertile and protected enough to foster the best kind of growth in kids as well as plants.

Given its position—both attached to the house, but separate from it as well—a yard is a place where watchful adult eyes are felt but not necessarily seen, a fact that allows kids a unique kind of protected freedom, rare in today's world.

Store-Bought Play Structures

An impressive array of play structures is available today, some so complete they look like small villages with swings, slides, monkey bars and elevated forts with canvas roofs, all connected in a single, well-designed and constructed unit. For the affluent or indulgent parent, these play structures are quite a temptation. The important question, however, is this: Do the kids like them?

Initially, you bet. What kid wouldn't? A play structure's well-thought-out design, however, seems to contain, unfortunately, a static, lifeless quality, which increases over time as the children become more familiar with it. It offers little room for children's imaginations to take over and customize the structure to suit their own needs. The thinking has all been done for them and,

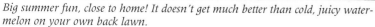

Big summer fun, close to home! It doesn't get much better than cold, juicy watermelon on your own back lawn.

Play structures not only provide good physical exercise for kids, they help develop their
imaginations as well.

This play structure is compact but leaves few
pleasures behind.

Who needs to go all the way to the playground when everything you need to have a good time
is right in your own backyard?

admittedly, done well.

Once they figure out that there's a definite limit to the type of fun that can be had with one of these units, however, kids tend to abandon them for more interactive arenas.

If the truth were known, most sophisticated play structures represent an adult's view of what a child should want. From a child's point of view, the best of all possible play areas would be an abandoned lot with lots of tall grass, a few big trees with perilously precarious limbs, lots of leftover lumber and empty cardboard boxes, and a full complement of tools to use (or misuse) in gleeful abandon. Just the thought of such a place sends most parents into paroxysms of horror.

A large, relatively flat playing surface is sometimes the best play "structure" of all.

Somewhere between the manufactured perfection of store-bought play structures and the wild and woolly allure of a vacant lot lies a happy medium, where both kids and adults will be content. A simple swing, an unadorned tree platform with a good rope ladder, and an old-fashioned sandbox—to name just a few—seem to fit the bill quite nicely.

One of the most important things any responsible adult can do to make a children's play area a little more safe is to make the "floor" as soft as possible. Ideally, the area under a tree fort, play structure or swing set should be covered with 4 inches or so of soft, shredded bark. As soft as a grass lawn may feel to bare feet, it's another thing altogether when someone slips from a swing.

As far as a sandbox goes, cats (your own or the neighbor's) will think it is nothing more than a king-sized cat box unless you take some measures to keep them out. One of the easiest sandboxes to build is a modest-sized container (4 feet by 6 feet is plenty big enough), using 2-inch by 12-inch lumber for the sides. Add a 2-inch by 6-inch cap around the perimeter, leaving a 1/2-inch reveal on the inside edge. Cut a piece of exterior-grade plywood to fit the opening (the reveal acts as a ledge, holding the plywood in place) and always cover the sandbox when it is not in use.

There are few things more fun than a backyard trampoline.

THE ULTIMATE SANDBOX

One of the biggest obstacles most sandbox owners face is how to keep cats from using it as a litterbox. These parents found a clever way of solving the problem by incorporating the sandbox into the design of their deck and including a cover that all but makes it disappear.

Built into this deck design is a sandbox that any toddler would love. The top of the box opens to reveal the play area.

With the top closed, the sandbox is protected from the weather, and the neighbors' cats (now what did we do with the kids?).

KIDS & GARDENS

Ask any adult gardener how they got started gardening and you'll probably hear a story that goes something like this: "When I was a kid, we lived next door to old Mrs. Smith, who had the most beautiful flower garden in her backyard I've ever seen. Even though I'm sure I was more of a pest than much help, she let me tag along with her in the garden."

Or maybe it was old Mr. Smith and his incredible veg-etable garden. Or a grandmother who let a youngster help dig new potatoes from the moist spring soil. Or an uncle who let a young niece eat tomatoes, warm from the vine, right out in the garden—complete with a salt

As long as adults have a good time working in the garden, kids will be eager to follow along.

shaker that magically appeared from the potting shed.

And then there are those avid adult gardeners who started out with nothing more than a fantasy garden, inspired, perhaps, by reading *The Secret Garden*.

"As the twig is bent, so grows the tree," says an old Chinese proverb. And so it seems with gardeners. Early childhood experiences in the green world hold the power to influence entire lives in the most delightful way imaginable.

If you think you might want to introduce a child to gardening, there are several secrets for success that you should take heed of (see sidebar at right). A little time and effort is all it takes to bring a lifelong gardener into the fold.

The garden world is a world unto itself, full of mystery and beauty—enough to last a lifetime.

CREATING A GARDENER: SECRETS FOR SUCCESS

Just Have a Good Time.

A writer and gardener by the name of Mary Jo Phillips once said the following: "The best way to encourage kids to garden is not to specifically encourage it. Making a big fuss over anything makes kids suspicious of your motives, so it rarely works. All you really have to do is be interested yourself. Then, a love of gardening and the natural world becomes a neat grown-up activity which you, of course, are kind enough to let them in on, instead of some deadly educational project."

This statement is certainly one secret to success when it comes to getting kids turned on to gardening. If you're having a good time doing something—whether it be cooking, fishing, knitting or gardening—chances are that kids are going to want to share in that good time.

Don't Work Too Hard.

Don't make gardening into work, especially initially. Weeding beds, mowing lawns and raking leaves can all come later. The first experiences should be fun and/or dramatic ones, like planting seeds, pulling carrots, hunting for four-leaf clovers or making a necklace from daisy flowers.

A Plot of Their Own.

If a child expresses an interest in gardening, let them have their own—small—garden plot. If the plot is too big, gardening will seem too much like work. Mark the plot as separate from the rest of the garden, and let the young gardener plant whatever it is they like to eat, even if it's just cucumbers and corn.

Use Fun Plants.

Go through a seed catalog with a youngster and point out all the weird or unusual plants you find. There's hardly an adult, let alone a kid, that wouldn't be interested in growing any of the following vegetables:

• 'Purple-podded' string beans that turn green when you put them in boiling water. They taste great too.

• There's also 'Plum Purple' radishes that mature in only 25 days from planting (that's less than a month!).

• 'White Wonder' tomatoes that are low in acid (which make them taste sweeter), productive and, yes, white.

• 'All-Blue' potatoes that taste like regular potatoes but are deep blue in color. How could you resist?

• 'Thumbelina' carrots that look like little orange Ping-Pong balls.

• 'Jack-Be-Little' pumpkins that are only 3 inches across or, at the opposite end of the spectrum, the 'Atlantic Giant' pumpkin, which can grow to over 600 pounds!

• 'Sunbeam' sunflower grows only 5 feet tall and has the loveliest bright green "eyes" you've ever seen. No kidding.

• 'Treasure Chest' celosia produces large, practically neon-colored crested flower heads resembling a cockscomb. Well, the catalog says the flowers look like cockscombs; your kids will say they look like brains. Trust the kids.

• Lunaria—otherwise known as the "money plant." Hard to imagine anyone who wouldn't want to plant it! Very easy to grow. Under their papery husks, the seed pods not only look like silvery coins, but contain seeds for planting next year. Talk about a payoff!

• 'Enormous Elephant's Ear' is a bulb that produces, just as it says, enormous green leaves that look just like elephant's ears.

• 'Moon Vine' looks a little like a morning glory, but the pure white, fragrant flowers open in the evening—in less than a minute! It's like watching time-lapse photography.

• 'Black Devil' pansies are truly black with a small orange dot at the center. What is it about black flowers that captures people's imagination?

• Sunflower 'Giganteus' is an old, easy-to-grow standby that can hardly help delight any gardener of any age. This variety is the big boy of the lot: flowers over a foot across on plants up to 10 feet tall! Kids love the seeds and so do the birds. A great addition to the garden.

GAMES FOR KIDS OF ALL AGES

With very few exceptions, every game we play today has its roots in ancient history. It seems that for as long as there have been humans in the world, there have been games.

The one aspect of games that has changed over the past several thousand years, is why we play them. When primitive people first started throwing rocks at a target, it was to sharpen their hunting skills, not to score points. When the ancients tossed the dried knucklebones of sheep (a precursor to the modern game of jacks), it was an attempt to foresee the future, not merely a way of passing time and increasing one's hand-eye coordination. And a tug-of-war between two communities a thousand years ago was not just for laughs, but for a sign from above, indicating whose rice harvest was going to be the best.

Today, the person looking for an excuse to play an outdoor game might be quick to point out the benefits of exercise and the lessons learned in any cooperative team effort. But the very fact that anyone would need an excuse to play a game, may itself be an indication of misplaced priorities.

Someone once said that the purest form of relaxation is play. If that observation is true, then perhaps game playing is every bit as significant for us today as it ever was in the past, albeit for different reasons. If the playing of a game of croquet, a family reunion tug-of-war or an extended session of flashlight tag on a warm summer night allows you, your family or your friends to slow down for a moment, enjoy the company of those around you and perhaps get in a good laugh or two, then game playing has an important place in contemporary life. Games, and the fun that goes with them, may provide the light-hearted focus and laughter we so desperately need as balance in a world of weighty concerns.

Play by the Rules?

Backyard games come in all degrees of sophistication, from croquet and badminton to hide-and-seek and flashlight tag.

PLAYING FOR FUN

One of the best aspects of backyard games—as opposed to games played at school and the world of professional sports—is that they can be played for no other reason than to have a good time.

All of us know certain people for whom simply having fun is a foreign concept. Put a racquet in one of these people's hands, and a barefoot game of badminton quickly takes on the gravity of an Olympic trial match. While it's true that competition is an intrinsic part of any game (even if you are playing a game by yourself), when it comes to backyard games the accent should definitely be on fun rather than competition. There are plenty of other places where strict competition has its rightful place; perhaps it's best to leave it there, rather than on your backyard lawn.

If kids are a part of your backyard, they'll definitely be party to the games played there. Kids, especially, need to know that all the world is not an arena, and that there are times when it's okay just to hang out, have fun and maybe even laugh at one's own mistakes. If you find yourself in the role of game facilitator or referee, a relaxed attitude on your part reinforces the notion of the backyard as a place to play rather than a stadium where winning is all. With just a little bit of positive reinforcement in the fun department, there will be a lot more laughter than whining and tears.

The best thing about any of these backyard games is also the worst—namely, a freewheeling disregard for the official rules and regulations. A fast-and-loose interpretation of the rules may make a game easier and livelier to play, but it can also cause problems when not everyone agrees with your interpretation.

Any organized game will be a lot more successful if played by some set of mutually agreed-upon rules; they may not be the rules in the book, but there should be at least an agreement on what the "house rules" are, no matter how customized or idiosyncratic they may be. This is especially important when the players span several generations. An adult who insists on a certain set of rules, even when confronted with a child's objection of, "But that's not the way we play it at camp … " will suddenly be seen as something less than a team player. So start any game with a definitive statement of whatever rules you want to follow. Doing so will clear the path to a lot more fun.

If you agree that the main point of any backyard game is to have a good time, considerable leniency can be allowed in all aspects of game playing. So what if your lawn is irregularly shaped and lumpy, or that you can't find one of the croquet balls and have to use a whiffle ball instead? The game of croquet will simply become that much more of a challenge and something to laugh over, rather than fret about.

All that said, here are descriptions of a variety of outdoor games you can play while living outdoors ... and basic rules for each.

Although it's easy enough for almost anyone to play, badminton provides a surprisingly strenuous workout.

Badminton

Badminton has one of the richest and most varied histories of any game played today. Historians know that a game very much like badminton was played in ancient Greece and Egypt. More important, the act of hitting a shuttlecock with some kind of racket has been almost universal since time immemorial—except that instead of it being a sport, the activity was used to foretell the future. The number of times one could hit the shuttlecock straight into the air without missing would indicate the number of spouses one would have, the number of years one might live and so forth.

Somewhere along the way, the soothsaying aspect of the shuttlecock and racket gave way to an organized game. And, like most good games, badminton eventually migrated to various corners of the world. In the 19th century, British army officers stationed in India took note of a game called poona (a game played with rackets and a shuttlecock) and took the game with them when they returned home. In 1873, poona was played on the grounds of the home of the Duke of Beaufort at Badminton, England. From that point on, the game was known as badminton.

Today, badminton is played in more than 70 countries worldwide. The International Badminton Federation oversees competitive matches. World Cup games are held every 3 years and, interestingly, are restricted to amateur players. Practice enough in your backyard and you could find yourself participating in a world-class competition!

Badminton is the only game played with a shuttlecock, a half of a round piece of cork (or some other substance, such as plastic or nylon) with feathers stuck in the flat end. Hit with the small, light racquet, the shuttlecock can travel straight through the air at speeds of more than 100 miles per hour and then suddenly slow down and drop to the ground. Although the game is very easy for beginners to pick up, the curious behavior of the shuttlecock makes badminton a challenging game for the most fit and agile of athletes.

Official badminton games are played indoors, usually on a wooden floor. Most would agree that it is a much more pleasant game when played outdoors, on a grass court. The official size for a badminton court is 17 by 44 feet, a size easily accommodated by most backyard lawns. For a doubles game (two players per side), the width of the court is expanded to 20 feet. The badminton net divides the center of the court. An official net is 20 feet long by 30 inches wide. The top of the net should measure exactly 61 inches from the ground.

Bocce

Bocce (or boccie, as it is sometimes spelled) is directly related to a similar game played in ancient Greece and Rome. The rules for bocce are so simple that any age group can play, but enough strategy and finesse are involved to keep it interesting day after day. Indeed, in many parts of Europe, you'll find the same group of people playing on public courts every day of the week, often in fierce competition.

Bocce is almost universally played on packed dirt or clay courts, some of which are filled with naturally occurring hazards like tree roots or immovable stones. Given this somewhat cavalier approach to the condition of the court, feel free to play bocce on the lawn, if you wish. The lawn will

Long popular in Europe, the pleasures of bocce are now known to Americans.

STORING EQUIPMENT

Playing a backyard game is often a spur-of-the-moment activity. And nothing dampens a whim faster than having to go search for the equipment or finding the supplies so ravaged that it's impossible to play the game. To avoid this, keep all of your backyard game supplies in one, easily accessible spot, even if it's just a large cardboard box kept in the garage.

Every once in a while it's a good idea to round up all the boxes the equipment came in, try to find the instruction booklets, and check to see if you have a full set of croquet mallets, usable shuttlecocks or a volleyball that still holds air. If there are missing pieces, carefully search the entire backyard. It's amazing how a badminton racquet will mysteriously appear from behind the shrubbery and how missing croquet balls show up, inexplicably, in the tree house. Scrupulously comb the lawn, because if there's one thing you never want to do, it's run over a horseshoe with a power lawnmower!

Several manufacturers have recently started making good-sized "lockers," usually constructed of molded plastic, expressly designed for the storage of items such as play equipment. Completely impervious to the effects of weather and watertight, to boot, these lockers can be conveniently stored out-of-doors, near the action, and then moved to an indoor spot, like a garage or porch, for the winter. Come the following spring, you can quickly get back into the swing of things, confidently knowing that all the necessary equipment is right there, all in one spot, ready to go.

produce a different kind of "action," but there's no rule that says you can't play bocce on a lawn.

Traditional courts are 12 by 60 feet long, although the measurements can be modified if the proportions are kept the same (such as 6 by 30 feet, or 8 by 45 feet).

The perimeter of a bocce court is usually defined with a short embankment (at least the height of a bocce ball, about 4 3/8 inches), sturdy enough to withstand being hit by a speeding ball. Long lengths of 2 by 6 lumber, well anchored to the ground, will do nicely. Proficient bocce players use the side and back walls for banking and rebound shots.

Bocce is played with eight large balls and one smaller target (or object) ball called the pallino. The game may be played one against one (four balls per person), with two two-person teams (two balls per person), two three-person teams (one ball per person), or with two four-person teams (one ball per person). The balls are made in two colors to distinguish the balls of one team from those of the other.

The object of the game is to throw your balls closer to the pallino than your opponents do.

Croquet

Croquet is a game that inspires great passion in some people. Fierce croquet matches held between families have been known to go on for generations, from one year to the next. It is a timeless game, one that can be as simple or as complex as the players care to make it.

Unlike most other games, croquet's exact origins are not known. What is known is that a game very similar to croquet, called paille maille, was played during the 1300s in France. It made its way to Ireland, and from there to England, where, interestingly, a London field where it was played is still known

by the English version of paille maille—namely, Pall Mall.

It wasn't until 1850 that the game became widely popular, when a London toymaker, John Jaques, manufactured a complete croquet set. Soon thereafter, Americans were introduced to croquet, and although over the last 100 years or so its popularity has waxed and waned, it has never completely

fallen out of favor. What was once a highly refined game intended for the elite has now become a common, pleasant backyard pastime and one of the fastest-growing games in America.

Tournament croquet is played on a rectangular grass court, mowed to a height of only 1/4 to 1/2 inch. Keeping professional croquet courts in perfect condition requires the

When played by the rules, croquet is a game that requires considerable finesse and skill.

same meticulous attention as putting greens. Obviously, home croquet courts can be more relaxed and the court any size you want. If possible, the long sides of the rectangular court should be twice as long as the short sides. And if a court 50 by 100 feet is not possible, 30 by 60 will do—a size most aficionados agree is as small as the court can be and still allow challenging play. If you don't have that much room, or if your lawn is of an irregular shape, decrease the number of wickets or set them up in any pattern you like.

The object of croquet is to hit your ball through the course of wickets in the prescribed order. The first person to hit the finishing stake wins the game.

Somewhere along the way, players must decide for themselves whether they are going to play croquet "by the book," or by some other, simplified set of "house rules." To avoid disagreement, make sure everyone agrees to the approach before the game begins.

Horseshoes

That old line—"close only counts in horseshoes and hand grenades"—isn't altogether true. Close also counts in bocce, jeu de boules, lawn bowls and a few other games here and there. Regardless of the accuracy of the statement, it does indicate that horseshoes is a game where precision isn't everything. Horseshoes is a game where the fun players have counts for at least as much as their points.

The game of horseshoes dates back to a similar game played by soldiers in ancient Rome. When the Romans conquered Britain, they took the game with them. From Britain, the game of horseshoes crossed the ocean to America with the early settlers and has been played in this country ever since.

The object of the game is to pitch the horseshoes so they are caught by the stake—a feat known as a "ringer." In addition to ringers, horseshoes 6 inches or closer to the stake are counted in a player's score.

An official horseshoe court requires a space 6 by 50 feet. Although it seems like a large area, many suburban lots can accommodate a horseshoe court in a side yard—an under-used space if there ever was one.

Played since ancient times, the game of horseshoes continues to hold appeal today.

Shuffleboard

Shuffleboard began as a type of street game played in England during the Middle Ages. It was known then as "shovel-board." Like most games, it went in and out of fashion (at one time during the 1600s it was relegated back to its humble beginnings and was primarily played in taverns), until someone got the idea to shorten the court (to 28 feet) and install it as a ship-board pastime in the late 1800s. By the early part of this century, a shuffleboard court became a standard feature on all ocean liners, seemingly ensuring the fashionable quality of this game for all time. The first outdoor shuffleboard courts in this country were built in 1913 in Florida. By 1929, the National Shuffleboard Association had been created, and did much to popularize the game by standardizing its rules and holding national tournaments, the first of which was held in 1931.

In the United States, a standard shuffleboard court is 52 feet long by 6 feet wide. The most common surface for the court is smooth concrete, but shuffleboard can also be played on wood surfaces, provided they are smooth enough to allow the pucks to slide unimpeded from one end to another. The actual playing area of the shuffleboard court is only 39 feet long.

More fun and complex than you might imagine, shuffleboard is once again gaining popularity.

HANDY TO HAVE ON HAND

It's no fun to have to run to the store to get that one missing something, especially when the trip necessitates a change of clothes, putting on shoes, and finding your wallet and keys just to get out the door. As the proprietor of your own back-yard game and sports complex, you can make life a lot easier by keeping the following items on hand:

- Small air pump
- Metal inflation needle
- Chalk for marking lines
- Extra shuttlecocks
- First aid kit
- Sunscreen
- Insect repellent
- Large, reusable plastic drink cups

If you have trouble keeping all the equipment needed for various games intact, keep your eyes open the next time you visit a garage sale. Someone else's incomplete badminton, croquet, bocce or horseshoe set may be just what you need to round your's out back home. Undoubtedly, the price will be right, and you may even wind up with enough mallets, balls and nets to invite the whole neighborhood over.

Volleyball

The American version of volleyball is an adaptation of a late 19th century German game known as Faustball. The Germans had, in turn, imported the game from Italy, where it had been played since the Middle Ages.

In 1895, the physical education director of the Young Men's Christian Association of Holyoke, Massachusetts, William G. Morgan, revised the German game and re-named it mintonette. Morgan originally conceived of mintonette as an indoor game, designed for older members of society who found other outdoor sports too strenuous—somewhat ironic, when today's beachfront game is considered.

Morgan's game of mintonette differed from Faustball in two important ways: first, the ball was not permitted to hit the floor (in Faustball, the ball could bounce twice before being returned), and second, instead of a rope stretched across the middle of the court, mintonette called for the use of a net. Morgan's changes have endured, but his name for the game has not. Noting the volleying nature of the game, Dr. Alfred Halstead (a colleague of Morgan's), suggested the name "volleyball," and so it has been ever since.

Equipment needed for volleyball includes only the volleyball itself, and a 30-foot-long, 3-foot-wide net, with poles and anchors for stretching tightly across the court. The net is placed across the middle of a 60- by 30-foot court, the top of the net measuring 8 feet above the ground.

Volleyball games can be played on almost any surface, but sand or grass is the best for cushioning falls—not uncommon in today's spirited game. Tournament games are played with six players to a side.

Only the serving team can score a point. The player at right back serves the ball while standing behind the baseline. The served ball must clear the top of the net and stay within the boundaries of the opposite side of the court. If the opposing side does not successfully return the ball over the net, in a maximum number of three hits, the serving side scores a point. If the server fails to serve the ball successfully, play goes to the opposite side, although no point is scored by the opposing team.

Never let the ball touch the ground inside your own court; doing so results in a point scored or a side-out for the opposing team. The first team to score 15 points is declared the winner. In the case of a 14 to 14 tie, the winner will be the first team to lead by two points.

There are three styles of serving the ball in volleyball: underhand, overhand and sidearm. While the underhand serve is the most popular and easiest to control, the overhand serve is considerably faster and harder to return, as is the sidearm serve, although to a lesser extent. It's best to start with the underhand serve, especially in competitive play, practicing the overhand or sidearm serve on your own. Once perfected, these two serves can be deadly to the opposition.

Generally speaking, a back-line player (known as a "stopper") receives the serve, hitting to a forward teammate (known as the "set-up" or "booster") who, in turn, sets up a high shot to be slammed into the opposing court by a neighboring front-line player, known as the "spiker." This slam shot requires leaping into the air and hitting the ball sharply with the heel of the palm, and is often unreturnable by the opposing team.

With the exception of plain old fumbles by the opposition, most points in volleyball are won by the offensive tactics of the spiker—that player in the front row who hammers the ball into the opposing court. To be most effective, the spiker should aim the ball into an unprotected "hole" on the opposing side. If the spiker has been properly set up by the booster—with a lofty ball 10 to 15 feet high, about a foot or so from the net—he or she should jump into the air as high as possible and slam the ball at a downward angle with great force. Varying this procedure also has its rewards, however. Many points have been won by a spiker who only pretends that the ball is about to be slammed, with great war-cries and much grimacing, and then merely taps the ball barely over the net. Imagine their surprise!

While spiked balls are difficult to return, they can be blocked by one or two receivers who jump up on the other side of the net, arms outstretched, palms open and together. This move not only takes guts, but timing—especially if two teammates try to do it in unison. The object, of course, is to simply meet the spiked ball "head-on" with your open palms, deflecting the speeding ball directly back over the net. Good luck.

JUNIOR VOLLEYBALL

The United States Volleyball Association has approved a variation of volleyball for junior players. Interestingly, it contains many of the rules from Mr. Morgan's original game of mintonette from way back there in 1895.

For junior volleyball, the net should be lowered to 7 feet, and the court reduced to 40 by 20 feet. The server has two tries to get the ball over the net, teammate assisted, if necessary. If desired, the server may also stand in the center of the back court for serving. After a successful serve, the ball can be hit as many times as is necessary to return it over the net. Individuals may hit the ball more than once in succession.

Ready for a good workout? Volleyball can provide just that, and with a minimum of equipment.

Index

Photo Credits

John Mowers/Mowers Photography pp.: cover, 14, 15, 20, 24(3), 39(3), 40(2), 41(3), 82, 84, 109(2), 139, 140; **Chuck Crandall and Barbara Crandall** pp.: 1, 2-3, 4, 5, 7, 8-9, 10 both, 11 both, 12, 13 both, 14, 15, 16, 16-17, 18 all, 19 both, 21 both, 22, 23, 24, 25, 26, 28 both, 29 both, 30, 31(3), 32 both, 33 both, 34, 34-35, 36, 37 all, 38(2), 39(4), 40(2), 41(2), 42, 43 all, 44, 44-45, 45, 46, 47, 48 all, 49, 54, 55, 56, 57 all, 58, 59 both, 60(2), 61 both, 62 all, 63, 64, 65 all, 66, 67(2), 68-69, 69, 70 both, 71 both, 72 all, 73, 74 all, 75, 76 both, 77 both, 78-79, 81(2), 82, 82-83, 83, 88, 106-107, 108 both, 109, 110 all, 111 both, 112, 113 all, 114, 115, 116, 117(5), 118 both, 119, 120-121, 121, 122 both, 123 both, 124, 125 all, 126, 128, 130-131, 131, 132, 133 both, 134-135, 135, 136 both, 137 all, 138-139, 140-141, 141(2), 142, 143 all, 144, 149 both, 150; **David Cavagnaro** pp.: 5, 12, 23, 31, 55, 60, 79, 80, 81(2), 84, 84-85, 85 both, 86 both, 87 both, 88(2), 90 all, 91 all, 92 both, 93(3), 94, 95 all, 96 all, 97(3), 98 both, 99 all, 100 all, 101(2), 102-103, 103, 104 both, 106, 115, 117, 119, 145; **Walter Chandoha** p.: 93; **NHGC Archive** p.: 97; **CCA Archive** pp.: 127, 129; ©**Joan Iaconetti/Bruce Coleman, Inc.** p.: 142; **Lawrence D. Migdale c/o Mira** pp.: 146-147; ©**Pat Bruno/Positive Images** p. 148; ©**Bill Bachman/Stock Boston** p.: 151; ©**D.P. Herskowitz/Hersh/Bruce Coleman, Inc.** p.: 153.

Illustrators

Nancy Wirsig McClure/NHGC Archive p.: 27 all; **Bryan Liedahl** pp.: 48, 50 all, 51 all, 52 all, 53 all, 55 all, 59, 73 all, 89(5); **Bill Reynolds** pp.: 75 all, 77 all, 89, 111 all.